Gary Brown

AFRICA

SAFARIS IN BOTSWANA AND ZAMBIA and TRAVELS THROUGH SOUTH AFRICA

Spring 2008

This journal was transcribed from the original hand-written journal maintained by Gary during his trip to Africa.

MONDAY, MAY 12

Linda and Gary on British Airway's flight from SeaTac to Heathrow

Linda and I have just settled into our business class seats on British Airline's 9:25 p.m. flight from Seattle to London; the first leg of our journey to Cape Town, South Africa.

Mike Sweeney brought us to SeaTac airport at 6:30 p.m. Linda and I got through security, sat and had drinks and dinner at an airport restaurant. After we finished we went to British Air's World Club Room at the airport to wait for our flight. While there, we bumped in to Mike and Michelle Mincy who are off to Italy for two weeks and are now seated just a row away on the plane. We were chatting about our flights and I offered Mike some of my Ambien to help him sleep. I handed the pills to him, he took them and then, acting alarmed, I said, "Oh no! Were those the Ambien---or the Viagra?!" That prompted the appropriate amount of laughter amongst all four of us and conversation about whether, during the flight, Mike would be sleeping, or "up" all night!

The plane is pushing back now. It is going to be a long journey; if everything is on schedule, 33 hours will have elapsed between the time we left our home and the time we arrive at our hotel in Cape Town!

TUESDAY, MAY 13

Heathrow Airport's new Terminal 5

Now it is late afternoon London time and I am sitting in Heathrow Airport in British Airway's World Club. I have been able to shower while here, read the paper and relax. Relax, that is, until I picked up the Kakuro puzzle in the Daily Telegraph. Damn, those puzzles are hard; too much thinking for me at this time!

I also had time to write this group email home:

> ***LONDON***
> ***Subject: First leg complete....***
>
> *Linda and I landed at London's Heathrow airport at 3:30 p.m. London time (7:30 a.m. Tuesday, Seattle time). We had a smooth, nine-hour, sleep-filled ride over the top of the world (Baffin Bay awaits you Bob & Cathy) to London. The sleep meds did their job. Heathrow's new Terminal 5 is very nice, although a half-hour bus ride from the rest of the terminals! I am feeling refreshed after a shower at British Airways World*

Club; it feels like this trip is just starting. Perhaps this long trip to Cape Town won't be so bad after all.

In Seattle we bumped into friends Mike and Michelle Mincy who are off on their first international trip to Italy. They ended up sitting near us on our flight to London. After talking about the duration of our trips I offered Mike some of my Ambien. When I pulled the pills out to give him a couple I jokingly said that I mix the Ambien in with the Viagra, so I hoped I was giving him the right pills. He said, "Oh well, I will either be fast asleep---or up---all night". Good attitude, Mike!

That's it for now. I don't want to keep any of you from the god-damned 80 degree weather!! Save a little for us.

Gary

The weather is beautiful in London today, as is this Terminal 5; Heathrow's highly acclaimed new terminal. However, from where we deplaned, we had at least thirty minutes of a winding bus ride through several tunnels through and around the airport to get here. But, it is pretty nice once you arrive!

The business class seats and a couple of Ambien did the trick getting here. I slept a pretty solid six hours of the nine hour flight. I neither ate nor drank on the flight; I am sure that helped, too.

After that sleep and the shower I just had, I am fresh and ready for the next leg to Johannesburg, South Africa, and then on to Cape Town. It must be eleven hours in the air, plus losing one hour, takes us from a 7 p.m. departure from London to a 7 a.m. arrival in Johannesburg. We are then scheduled to leave at 10 a.m. on our flight from Johannesburg to Cape Town, getting in there shortly after noon.

Time to go to the gate.

WEDNESDAY, MAY 14

Victoria Wharf in front of Victoria & Albert Hotel in Cape Town

I am in Cape Town. It is 5 p.m. I am sitting in the Victoria & Albert Hotel's bar. I am showered, in clean clothes; tired, but not exhausted, or at least I am not feeling that way at the moment.

It was an uneventful flight from Heathrow to Johannesburg. The bad news is that Linda's luggage apparently never emerged from Heathrow's brand-new, trouble-fraught Terminal 5. British Air thinks they will be able to get the missing bag to us sometime tomorrow. Fortunately, Linda carried some of her hair stuff in her carry-on backpack.

A funny side-note about the backpack Linda is using as her carry-on. She borrowed it from Jaret who, unbeknownst to Linda, had left a screwdriver in the bag. Seattle's security caught it. It must have been Linda's look of shock and then laughter that caused the security folks to allow her to keep it. I was surprised!

At Johannesburg's airport a messenger from Pulse Africa (the agency we used to help us arrange our safaris) met us to give us our travel vouchers for the safaris. They also gave us a real nice travel satchel. The messenger walked us over to the domestic terminal where we caught our 10 a.m. flight to Cape Town. Nice service.

I was surprised at how barren the landscape is as we flew across South Africa. Much of the terrain was treeless and not farmed, maybe because it isn't farmable.

At Cape Town airport, we picked up what luggage we had (mine) and picked up our Avis rental car. With the steering wheel on the wrong side of the car I managed to drive on the wrong side of the road all the way to our hotel. I also managed to turn the windshield wipers on twice before even getting out of the airport. Does it make sense they put the turn signal on the wrong side of the steering column, too?

We got to the Victoria & Albert Hotel from the airport easy enough and got checked into our room, which is really quite nice. Linda had to have a piece of pizza to quell her stomach and then we took off in the car again to drive to the cable car that takes you to the top of Table Mountain. It was closed; the winds were too strong, although they didn't seem so at the bottom. I gather they were anticipating stronger winds and didn't want to have a bunch of people on top when the strong winds arrived, which they did about an hour ago. In fact, it is starting to get downright stormy outside at the moment.

Since we weren't able to take the cable car to the top of Table Mountain, we just drove around for a while. Cape Town is really quite beautiful; I am just too tired to comment on it right now.

I think I will take a break to make plans for tomorrow.

THURSDAY, MAY 15

Table Mountain and its cable car in Cape Town

It is about 8 a.m. and I am having coffee at the Victoria & Albert Hotel in Cape Town. Linda and I left the car in the lot and stayed near the hotel last night; we walked along the waterfront looking for a place to eat. We stopped at a nice looking bar/restaurant for a glass of wine while we decided where to eat.

The place we went into claimed to be the largest wine bar in the world. It had maybe 50 wines by the glass. We stayed with South African wines and enjoyed a couple of different glasses of their red. We got advice from Thomas, the bar tender, and ordered Linda a good Pinotage, which is a blend of Pinot Noir and Hermitage (a Syrah). While at Flying Fish in Seattle one night, Britt, Mike and I didn't much care for the only Pinotage I had ever tried, but Linda had loved it. So, she and I thought she should try another. It still tastes odd to me (excuse me, but Pinot Noir shouldn't be blended---just sayin'); Linda didn't much care for it this time, either.

We got into a conversation with a nice South African couple from Cape Town. They gave us advice about things to do and places to eat before they had to leave us to join a larger group. Linda and I ended up eating dinner at that wine bar and got back to our hotel about 10:30 p.m. We were surprised to have lasted that long.

We both slept like babies. I didn't wake up until 7:30 a.m. I was very surprised to sleep so late; not that I wanted to. I had hoped that leaving the drapes open would wake me with the morning sun, but that apparently failed! Likely because it is a gloomy day here so far, although it looks like it could burn off. The top of Table Mountain is ensconced in clouds.

— — —

It is now about 6:30 p.m. and we are sitting at the Victoria & Albert Hotel's bar. We didn't leave the hotel this morning until after 10:30. So, it was a short day, but a good one.

When we left the hotel we drove out to the Cape of Good Hope and Cape Point by going along False Bay (the Indian Ocean side) and coming back into Cape Town along the Atlantic Ocean side. The Cape of Good Hope is the southwestern-most point of Africa, but not the southern-most. That honor goes to Cape Agulhas 125 miles east (and a little south) of the Cape of Good Hope.

The entire Cape peninsula is gorgeous; rugged rock precipices and windblown. It was a great drive; we got back into Cape Town and our hotel about 4:30 p.m.

I guess by most measures you would have to call my day complete: I watched both an African Penguin couple and a baboon couple mate today! Could it get any better?!

As we drove south out of Cape Town this morning, we cut across the peninsula behind (east of) Table Mountain to Muizenberg on False Bay. We then drove along the water to Fish Hoek and then to Simon's Town. The road, and these little towns, cling to the lower hillside under sheer cliffs of the rock mountain towering behind them. It was very scenic.

We stopped at Boulder just beyond Simon's Town to see the resident African Penguin clan. The area is a reserve so the penguins are protected, but you are able to walk out among them on walkways. One of the little guys waddled up so close to me as I was kneeling down taking his picture, I thought he might peck my camera lens. I should have some great pictures of him, twisting and cocking his head in curiosity. These penguins mate for life and we watched various pair interact, nuzzling each other, preening each other, and like I said earlier, having sex with each other. These penguins are also called Donkey Penguins because they bray to establish territory. It was captivating watching this colony interact socially. I watched them for quite a while. It was very interesting.

From Boulder, we continued south to the end of the peninsula to the two capes. Despite the fact that it has the world-famous name and a little plaque saying it is the southwestern-most point in Africa, the

Cape of Good Hope is not as impressive as Cape Point. The two capes are in sight of each other. Cape Point has a funicular to its top, but we didn't bother taking it.

On the drive back to the north, we ran into a troop of baboons on the road. It was a troop of maybe 12. One dominant male (he is the one that scored), several females (one of which was the scoree) and some babies (the result of past scores). Once again, it was interesting watching these animals interact socially. Particularly the dominant male. He was very watchful and kept his troop together; he was big, powerful and not so friendly. When some female tourist got out of her car (not very smart), the male immediately moved over to put himself between her and his troop. He would not have taken kindly to her moving any closer; she may have found out what the signs along the road meant when they said baboons can be very dangerous.

Most all of the peninsula is a national park, which accounts for the wildlife we saw while driving around it. We drove back to Cape Town along the Atlantic coast. Between Noordhoek and Hout Bay is Chapman's Peak Drive, acclaimed as one of the world's prettiest drives. No argument here; it is amazing! Built between 1910 and 1920 it is an engineering marvel; it is

literally etched into the cliff-side over the pounding waves of the Atlantic Ocean.
Linda spent most of her day during our drive agonizing over her lost luggage; making phone calls to British Air. It is still not clear when, or even if, she will get her bag. When we got back to the hotel this afternoon, I explored the wharf; Linda went shopping.

While tooling around the wharf, I got our tickets for our trip tomorrow to Robben Island and walked through the exclusive Cape Grace Hotel. Then I went back to our hotel room, read the guidebook some, showered and got to the hotel bar where I am now a little after 6 p.m. Linda just joined me.

Sitting here at the bar, we are able to use the laptop the hotel provides and connect to the internet through their Wi-Fi. Linda has spent most of the time on the British Airway site writing emails saying God knows what to God knows who. By the time she is done with them, the airlines will wish they had never heard of her! When it was my turn to use the laptop, the battery was low so I wrote only a truncated group email home:

CAPETOWN, SOUTH AFRICA
Subject: Cape Town is Gorgeous!

Yes, we arrived safely and reasonably on time.

Unfortunately, of the four of us travelling together--me, my bag, Linda (no, those latter two are not one and the same) and Linda's bag--only three of us arrived in Cape Town. Much to Linda's consternation, her bag took a liking to Heathrow's new Terminal 5 and is still hanging out there. Most of you know what a "Linda Tizzy" is; British Airways is just learning! Watch the papers, BA may soon switch to cargo only.

Had a great first day in Cape Town. My trip is already complete. I watched African Penguins AND Baboons copulate today! How does it get better?

Oh oh...gotta go, juice is running out on this 'puter....will write again soon

Gary

FRIDAY, MAY 16

Robben Island – Entrance to the prison

It is 7:15 a.m. and I am sitting in the café at the Victoria & Albert Hotel having coffee. The sun has just risen and the day looks much like yesterday; Clouds moving through (probably covering Table Mountain, but I am not in a position to tell), fairly calm and 65 degrees. It is supposed to warm to 75 degrees later. I take off for Robben Island at about 8:30 a.m.; Linda has decided not to go with me.

Last night, Linda and I left the hotel about 7:30 p.m. and drove to Cape Town's old town along Long Street; we were headed to Mama Africa's, a traditional South African place popular with locals and visitors.

At Mama Africa's I had a great conversation with Hans from Belgium. He was a mid-thirties guy who is captain of an oil/natural gas ship. He takes off today in his 1,000-foot-long ship bound for Trinidad. His schedule is three months on, and three months off, a schedule he says his girlfriend isn't real keen of. He gave me his email address. After he left Linda and I talked with a number of black Africans; the local black African band had started playing and the locals were coming in to listen. We had a lot of fun joking around with them.

For dinner I had a mixed grill with crocodile, ostrich, kudu and springbok. The kudu was a little tough, but the other three were very, very good. I wore the left-over croc around my waist and put the last ostrich feather in my hat.

A couple from Atlanta has been talking to me at breakfast this morning. She originally came over and asked me how to convert Celsius to Fahrenheit. She wrote my simplified formula down. Then we started talking about lost luggage and safaris. They take off tomorrow for the Okavango and will be on safari for nine days.

— — —

Ah, Friday evening, 6 p.m. Beer time at the "Hotel Saloon"! I am dragging a little, I didn't sleep a wink from 2 a.m. on this morning. The 90-minute nap I just had helped, but I should sleep well tonight.

My journey today to Robben Island was just amazing. After reading Nelson Mandela's autobiography, "A Long Walk to Freedom", I was pretty knowledgeable about the things I saw and heard. But hearing from three different former political prisoners from Robben Island definitely had its impact.

I rode over on the ½ -hour ferry to Robben Island with a man I overheard was a prisoner for fifteen years. I tried listening in on one of his conversations. He was traveling with a group of friends, but the wind and his accent prevented me from catching much of what he was saying. I snuck a picture of him on the boat. It turned out, he was a

true celebrity: Eddie Daniels. Eddie was imprisoned with Nelson Mandela and had crafted a plane for Nelson to escape the island. But, the plan was turned down by the then leaders of Nelson's party, the ANC, as too dangerous. Another of Eddie's claims to fame, is that he went into prison with a sixth grade education and came out with two college degrees.

Our first guide on the Robben Island tour was on the bus where we spent most of our two-hour tour. He was imprisoned for ten years on Robben Island. During the tour, when he saw Eddie talking to his private group at the lime quarry, he filled us in about Eddie---and then asked him to come onto our bus to say hello to us. Eddie spoke for a few minutes. Everyone applauded. He was gracious and appreciative of us and all the visitors to the island. After hearing the guides' different talks about Robben Island, in general, and about Eddie in particular, Eddie's visit on our bus had a visible impact on all of us.

After touring around the island with our guide seeing the various buildings, the lime quarry, and other sights, we got off the bus to walk through the prison buildings and yard where the political prisoners, including Nelson and Eddie, were imprisoned. Nelson for 18 years, although he spent another 9 in another prison on the mainland.

Our guide for this portion of the tour was a five-year prisoner. He was younger and didn't start his prison term until the mid-80's; as he says, after much prison reform had occurred. Nelson was 46 years old when he first got to Robben Island in 1964 (he got out of the second prison in 1991 and was elected Prime Minister in 1994), and the prison conditions were much worse.

Both guides we had were amazingly well-spoken and both showed tremendous humility and balance in their talks. They made clear that the "movement" was not black verses white (not in their eyes, but it clearly was in the eyes of the government) and that there were many whites who fought, served and died serving the cause.

In short, it was an incredibly fulfilling tour for me. I got back to the hotel around 12:30 p.m.

Linda spent the morning shopping for replacement clothes. Little more seems to be known about her luggage today than the first day. She and I had lunch after I got back from Robben Island and then I went to the Two Oceans Aquarium, which is rated as one of the world's best. I thought it was just good, but then what do I know about aquariums?

I am not hearing much Afrikaans spoken or any native language, like Zulu. There are, though, eleven languages spoken in Cape Town, but clearly most folks must have English in their repertoire.

South Africa has some unique signage. While driving around Cape Town I noted several warning signs for "Panel Pounders", which is how they apparently refer to auto body repair shops. And I was a little concerned when I couldn't figure out what to beware of when I kept seeing road-warning signs saying "Robot". Once I gave up looking for R2D2, I realized that is the word they use here for a traffic light.

Using the hotel's laptop while sitting here in the bar, I wrote an email home. What a great way to do it; I would write a lot more emails home (and probably not hand-write my journals) if I could sit in a bar having a beer every night after a day of sight-seeing! Here is the email I sent home:

CAPETOWN, SOUTH AFRICA
Subject: Those damn Brits.....

It seems like all I talked about in the last couple of postings is Viagra and animal happenings....I will try to make this one more interesting.

Nearly all of the Cape Town peninsula is National Park, which explains in part all the wildlife we saw while driving around it. For you who care, by the way, the Cape of Good Hope is NOT the southernmost point of the continent of Africa, it is the southwestern-most. The award for southernmost goes to a Cape about 125 miles east....and slightly south....of here. The whole peninsula, which extends maybe 20 miles south of Cape Town, is remarkably pretty: the road and small towns squeezed between the water and towering rock cliffs jutting to the clouds. The most prominent and well-known of these is Table Mountain which stands guard over Cape Town itself.

If we all have nothing else to be thankful for, let's all take a moment to appreciate the fact we removed ourselves from Britain's influence before the automobile. Putting the steering wheel on the right side and then driving on the wrong side of the road is as unnatural as walking backwards, or for a right-hander to pick his nose with his left hand. It just isn't proper! And yes, Murray, I will pay attention to which hand you use. The only thing they got right was not screwing around with the pedals! Thank God they didn't mess with those. I am about to wear out a pair of windshield wipers trying to signal my intention to turn.

Linda's bag is still incognito, with little hope for relief. Linda's tizzy turned into a Linda shopping spree today. I *figure that British Air and Linda are colluding on this one. We just happen to be near South Africa's (maybe Africa's) largest shopping mall....and Linda just happens to lose her bag? Riiigghht! The pain got worse when she informed me tonight that BA would cover only $1,000 of her cost. Ooops that was 1,000 Euro. Ouch.*

While Linda shopped I spent the morning on Robben Island. Wow. It was honestly a moving and rewarding day for me. With the background I gained from having just finished Nelson Mandela's autobiography, "A Long Walk to Freedom", and the personal stories told by the guides who were former political prisoners at Robben Island, it was a very rich experience. An unexpected highlight was that Eddie Daniels just happened to be on my ferry visiting the island. Eddie was one of Nelson's prison mates and is famous for having concocted an escape plan for Nelson (turned down by the then party leaders of the ANC as too dangerous) and for having entered the prison with a 6th grade education and leaving with two college degrees. Each of the two former-prisoner-guides and Eddie were humble in relating their story and describing their experiences.

Off to try to sneak into a restaurant that has no room for us and won't like the way we are dressed...typical American tourists!!

Gary

SATURDAY, MAY 17

Roiling surf below Chapman's Peak Drive near Cape Town

This is starting out as a beautiful day! I am sitting in the breakfast room of the Victoria & Albert Hotel at about 8 a.m. and I can see all of Table Mountain and Devil's Peak. Not a cloud in the sky. I hope it stays this way for the day so we can get to the top of Table Mountain. I got a great night's sleep and I am energized by the sun!

We are nearing the shortest day of the year here (well, it's a month away) and the sun doesn't rise until 7:15 a.m. The light into our hotel room isn't waking me up until 7:30 or 7:45 in the morning; later than I want. Maybe I will start using the alarm.

We sat at the hotel bar last night until 7:30ish before driving again to Long Street. This time we went to an Italian Restaurant. It was very nice and had a great feel to it. Linda had ostrich and I had Cape Salmon, which is actually a white fish meat. Both were very good. Our five table neighbors were from the U.S.: Boise, Wyoming and California. They are also off to the Okavango for safaris.

Parking in Cape Town is interesting. There are a number of reflective-vested "parking officials" milling around the curbside of every street. If there is a space, they direct you to it, help you park and walk away. When you go to leave, they are there with their hand out. I don't know if these are "crooked" city employees, or if it is the way it is supposed to be. Surely, it is the norm in the evening, legal or not. During the day all of those guys are replaced in huge numbers by parking officials who write parking tickets---they swarm the city. It doesn't make sense. You would think violators would learn, or maybe the city needs to increase the deterrent by increasing the fine. Like I said, it doesn't make sense.

Linda's new "replacement" shoes were killing her so I walked to get the car after dinner to pick her up at the restaurant. By then, 10 on Friday night, parking (even with the "parking officials") was difficult so instead of venturing to another location in old-city we drove back to the wharf area at the hotel. We then walked to the place we were our first night, the wine bar I now know to be called Balthazar. The name of the restaurant is the name of the huge wine bottle that holds 12 liters (18 normal-size bottles).

Our conversation with Marlin, our bartender at Balthazar, induced him to set samples of various red wines in front of Linda and me to taste. The restaurant's owner and sommelier, John, was sitting at the end of the bar and overheard us talking; he came and joined us. John is from Plettenberg Bay, South Africa, and is two years into his study to become a sommelier. He poured us some Pinot Noir from George, a town east of Cape Town that we will be driving through in a few days. He suggested we should stop at the winery (Herold Wines) and talk with Fiona, the owner. I got the impression he was as interested in Fiona as he was her wines. We had a fun time with him and Marlin. We got back to our room around midnight.

It seems like we say this everywhere we go (which wouldn't be a bad thing): the locals, in this case the South Africans, are extraordinarily friendly and helpful. We both have had numerous experiences and interactions; too many to relate. It sure makes it pleasurable being here, which is the common theme: everyone seems genuinely concerned that you enjoy yourself while here.

— — —

The third time was not a charm. This morning, for our second effort, the cable car to the top of Table Mountain was temporarily down for technical reasons. When we returned later this afternoon for our third effort, the cable car was shut down for maintenance until Monday. So, we will not be riding to the top of Table Mountain on this trip.

It was a mess this morning in the area where you catch the cable car. Hundreds of people milling around waiting for the cable car to bet fixed and the masses of tour buses were blocking the ingress and egress of other vehicles---a real zoo. No one was telling anyone, including us, that the cable car was down, so more and more cars and buses kept trying to file into the impossible mess. We finally got ourselves extricated and drove away thinking we would come back later in the day. Had we waited it would have been a several hour wait. We had better things to do!

We found our way through Cape Town and drove around the east side of the base of Table Mountain to Constantia. It was a pretty drive. There are trees (Pines, maybe?) around the base of Table Mountain that are way cool, but I haven't yet been in a situation to get a good picture of them.

Constantia appears to be a fairly exclusive area; gated estates and neighborhoods and equestrian trails throughout. We stopped at Groot Constantia, the estate of the first Dutch governor in 1691, which became a rather famous winery in the 1800's. The buildings, grounds and vineyards are beautiful. The vines are in their "winter wear" and the brown, yellow and green colors are amazing; I hope they photographed well. We walked the grounds and sat and had some tea in the morning sun.

Prior to pulling into Groot Constantia we swung into the parking lot of the Kirstenbosch National Botanic Gardens, but moved on once we figured out that seeing the gardens would take longer than we wanted.

After Groot, we drove to and around Klein Constantia, the winery which produces one of the best cabernets of the country. We simply enjoyed the scenery; no wine tasting for us.

We then drove to Pollsmoor Prison where Nelson Mandela served his last nine years in prison before his release. I couldn't see where exactly, but he was confined in a house on or near the prison grounds.

We continued driving south over the mountain pass and through the Silver Mine Nature Reserve before connecting to the road near Noordhoek where we were two days ago. Now that we were on the Atlantic side of the peninsula, we turned north to view Long Beach and to take the Chapman's Peak Drive, for a second time, on our way back to Cape Town. There was some excitement at one of the pull-outs along Chapman's Peak Drive overlooking Long Beach. A couple of locals from Hout Bay were riding their bikes and noticed an emergency flare over the water. A Coast Guard helicopter was circling the beach looking for someone, or something, apparently in distress. Nothing was found while we watched.

The locals told us that the tide was very high (covering much of the huge sand beach we had seen two days earlier) and the surf was huge. The surf pounding the rocks along the drive on this otherwise bright, sunny day was quite dramatic.

I dropped Linda off at our hotel around 2 p.m. and took off again in the car. I wasn't done exploring yet. The first thing I did was to drive to the cable car again---this was my futile third effort---and then I drove into Bo-Kaap, Cape Town's Muslim Quarter. I was unsuccessful in my half-assed attempt to find the spice market in Bo-Kaap, but I did manage to get myself into some areas I really shouldn't have been in. I was trying to find my way to Signal Hill. In doing so, I drove through what was possibly someone's farm yard; pigs, geese and chickens milling around on the dirt street I found myself on. The whole while I noted black faces glaring at me. I made sure the doors were locked and did not stop to take pictures! It is a good thing Linda wasn't with me!

I got back to our hotel around 4 p.m., stuck my head into the hotel's gym, figuring that would suffice for a workout, and then went walking around the waterfront. The waterfront was very busy on this warm, sunny Saturday afternoon with street entertainers playing music, dancing and doing tricks.

I went back to our hotel room around 5 p.m., read about South Africa's wine country (tomorrow's adventure) and listened to the street music through the hotel's open windows. I nodded off until Linda returned from yet another shopping trip. I woke, showered and went with Linda downstairs to the hotel bar where I am now. I used the hotel's laptop to check emails and have been catching up in my journal, which I have now done!

SUNDAY, MAY 18

The Franschhoek Valley

Pounding thunder woke us up this morning. No rain here at the waterfront in Cape Town, but we heard from some bikers just now that they got pretty wet on the other side of Table Mountain earlier this morning. It is 10 a.m. and I am sitting in the Victoria & Albert Hotel's café.

It was another late morning for me. I got up to the sound of thunder at 7:45 a.m. and went to the hotel's gym to get a real workout in (from which I have yet to cool off in this muggy weather), showered, packed and had breakfast with Linda. Now, I am still in the café while Linda went off to buy a converter. When she gets back, we will start our drive east to the wine-lands and to Franschhoek, where we will spend the next two nights.

Last night, after I caught up in my journal sitting in the hotel's bar, Linda and I used the hotel's computer to Google the animals we have been eating: kudu, springbok and wildebeest. Next week, I am sure we will be seeing these in real life. We also emailed Britt knowing she is probably planning a big party at our house on Saturday night. We heard it was 80 degrees in Seattle; it was midmorning Saturday in Seattle, so we thought we might catch her at her computer. No response. She was probably outdoors enjoying the weather.

For dinner we decided to just walk down the waterfront to find a place to eat rather than to get into the car. We strolled into a restaurant with an attractive bar and sat there for drinks and dinner. We first talked to Todd from California who travels the world for his business (something to do with wine or beer). Nice guy with a family of a wife and three teenage daughters at home who he must not see much of. We had a chuckle with him as he shook his head telling us how his gorgeous (and she is, he showed us a picture) 19-year-old daughter tells him he needs to "chill out and have a bowl".

I was talked into (gladly) ordering the "Royal Platter" for 1,250 Rand ($166 US). It had a collection of various crayfish, prawns, and some critter from Madagascar, which is purportedly some combination of a crayfish and prawn. It was a huge platter, as it should have been, and the various shellfish were very good. It was expensive, but fun.

After dinner, we had a great conversation with a South African couple (he actually is a white Brit; she, a black lady from a town near Cape Town). They both work at an asphalt company, her as an accountant. We had lots of fun talking about both South African and U.S. politics. They were amazed I know so much about South African history and a little embarrassed I seemed to know more than they did. We were amazed at how much they knew about U.S. politics and were a little embarrassed they seemed to know more than us. We left them about midnight to return to our room.

This morning at breakfast with Linda I talked to a couple of bike riders. I had seen them yesterday, too, both times sitting having coffee. I told them I liked the way they rode bikes! Stopping here for coffee is their traditional break during their 85 kilometer (52 mile) ride. There are quite a few bikers here. The rides are gorgeous, but risky. The roads are narrow to begin with and rarely have shoulders. And then, you have tourists, like me, who are gawking around and aren't used to driving on the wrong side of the road. Like I said, risky.

Okay, time to go find Linda and get this wine-land show on the road!

— — —

It is now early evening and I just bellied up to the wine bar at the Hotel Le Franschhoek (means "French corner") three kilometers outside the village of Franschhoek. This will be our hotel for the next two nights.

We left Cape Town this morning a little after ten. We drove due east on the N-1 toward the heart of South Africa's wine country.

Our first stop was Paarl, the town in the first of the three wine valleys making up the wine-lands of South Africa.

Paarl itself is mostly uninteresting; nice and clean but undistinguished. It took about an hour to get there from Cape Town including a rather lengthy stop for gas. The gas attendants asked if we wanted them to clean the bird crap covering most of the hood and top of our rental car. It had been there since the first night when it got parked under a tree. Using window washers and a bucket of water, the attendants pretty much washed the entire car. They seemed pleased with the 23 Rand ($3 US) tip I gave them.

We drove through Paarl and then looped around along back roads for forty kilometers to get to the well-known wine area of Stellenbosch, the village of the second wine valley. The terrain near Stellenbosch was prettier than around Paarl; jagged rocks pushing up a couple thousand feet from the valley floor (they call them mountains here). The town itself is second only to Cape Town as the oldest in South Africa. It has a great "antique" feel to it and has the oldest Afrikaner university; lots of college kids milling around.

We stopped and listened with amusement as three co-eds argued amongst themselves how to answer our question about where Dorp Street was. Despite their good-natured haggling, they gave us good directions, except that we failed to follow them precisely and wandered around in the car longer than necessary.

We parked and strolled around Dorp Street. We had iced tea and cokes at a little café next too Oom Samie Se Winkel, a very curious curiosity shop, with garters hanging from the ceiling, warthog heads on the walls and every imaginable and unimaginable thing for sale. I can't imagine who would buy anything there!

It was very pleasant hanging out in Stellenbosch. The day was high overcast with occasional sun bursts and warm. A good day to just hang.

We left Stellenbosch and drove east and north over the Franschhoek Mountains into the third and final wine valley in which Franschhoek sits, twenty kilometers away.

As we worked our way over the little mountain pass, the scenery became stunning. Franschhoek is nestled in a horse shoe of towering rock edifices and the valley floor is matted with vineyards and grand wineries. The vineyards

have donned their vivid fall colors and are lined with fence lines and dotted with white winery buildings. All of this is set against the back drop of ragged and rugged mountains. They sure know how to make rock mountains here. I hope my pictures capture the beauty of this place. The wineries along the road were palatial with stunning grounds, dramatic gateway entrances and grand driveways. As pretty a winery setting as we have seen anywhere.

And, there must have been a hundred bed and breakfasts in and around the village of Franschhoek, which is quite quaint. We stopped there for a very late lunch at a bistro around 3 p.m.

I just moved to sit outside at the wine bar here at the Hotel Le Franschhoek. It is 6:30 p.m. and I want to enjoy this gorgeous evening, although darker here and writing will be more difficult.

Linda and I telephoned Britt and Mike earlier to tell them how comfortable our beds have been and how well the showers have worked. They didn't have such luck on their recent trip to Greece; we had to rub it in. We thought they would appreciate that!

So far, the South African drivers have been very civil; no horn honking, just like in Seattle. The roads are good, too. Except when I got off in "adventure land" yesterday in Bo-Kaap, road surfaces have been equal to American standards. The streets and roads of the peninsula were narrow, winding and without shoulders, but their national highways are divided, limited access and well-marked. The equivalent of our state and county roads are not quite as good as in the U.S., but very adequate. Except for driving on the wrong side of the road---which I have been remembering to do almost without fail---the driving here has been very easy so far.

The rooms and grounds of the Hotel Le Franschhoek are very nice. We walked around, took pictures and stopped by the spa. While Linda used the restroom at the spa, a very cute, petite black female therapist gave me a tour of it. Her enticing descriptions of her massages tempted me, but then she said she was done for the day! Tease.

After such a pleasant day, it is now starting to rain with a slight breeze. Linda and I are sitting outside on the hotel wine bar's porch under canvas awnings; the tattering of rain sprinkles striking the canvas. It is nice.

MONDAY, MAY 19

Gary & Linda having lunch in Franschhoek

It is a beautiful morning in Franschhoek. I have been sitting on the hotel's porch (the same place we sat last night) having coffee and reading the Cape Town newspaper. I wanted to go for a walk with Linda this morning, but she had to shower first---go figure. So what do I do? I drink coffee, read the paper, shower and eat an omelet! A long ways away from an exercise walk! Maybe this afternoon.

It's now about 9:30 a.m.; I initially got out here about 8 a.m. I am sitting here listening to the various pastoral sounds of the countryside: doves cooing, a rooster cock-a-doodling, birds chirping, tractor cleats clanging in the distance, the occasional hammering across the valley. Great morning.

After finishing in my journal last night and before leaving the hotel to drive to the village of Franschhoek to eat, Linda and I sat under the canvas cover of this porch and played gin while the rain pelted the canvas overhead. After playing twenty or so hands, we ended one point apart (me ahead, yes!).

We went to the village around 7:30 p.m. and went to Reuben's, a place that told us by phone that they had no room for us. We went anyway thinking maybe we could sit at the bar if they had one. The place was basically empty when we got there so they seated us right away. While the place did eventually fill up, it never got full. I am thinking the dishwasher answered the phone earlier and wanted to discourage us from coming to dirty more dishes!

Our meals at Reuben's were fantastic. Linda had pork belly and I had calf's liver. I wanted something more exotic, like gemsbok balls or something, but they only had springbok rump. The liver was the best I have ever had. And as we have found most everywhere, the service was friendly and accommodating.

It was early (nine-ish) when we finished dinner. The village was very quiet at this time on a Sunday night in their off-season. It was suggested we go to the Elephant & Barrel, a pub. It was a good suggestion since it was likely the only place open. The rain ended before we got to Reuben's, but the streets were still wet. At the Pub we had beer and wine and we called Britt. It must have been the alcohol because we had just talked to her! We got back to the hotel around 10:30 p.m.

— — —

It is now about 5:30 p.m. and Linda and I have come to sit on the porch of our hotel again---and boy, is it beautiful out right now. A simply gorgeous evening.

After our leisurely morning this morning (Linda and I ate breakfast together on the porch), we hopped into the car around 10 a.m. and drove off to visit some of the many wineries in the valley. We drove around casually stopping here and there, visiting wineries, taking photographs, talking to people, getting lost---and not drinking/tasting any wine. That is what evenings are for! We got back to the hotel around one in the afternoon.

Franschhoek was settled by the Dutch in 1688 and is one of the oldest settlements in South Africa. It still retains its Dutch influence. “Moanin’ suh”---typical morning greeting. “Plezhuh”---typical response to “thank you”. Great local idioms, like the word “brilliant” in response to just about anything by our British friends, James and Melissa who we met in Belize.

I changed clothes and went for an hour-long walk into the hills around the hotel---a power walk. I saw some cool things and worked up a good sweat in this unseasonably warm weather. We are hearing from locals that this 70-80 degree weather is unheard of here this time of year---lucky us! This day could hardly have been better weather-wise.

While I was gone walking, Linda was on the phone with British Air---again---learning that they will get her luggage to her in a few days when we are in Johannesburg. She is pretty happy. I hope they don’t disappoint her.

We went down to the village for a late lunch and to check out a place for dinner tonight---and for a place to have the wine we didn't have all day. While at lunch we learned from the waitress that it is a 700 kilometer drive to Plettenberg Bay, where we head tomorrow. That will be 7-8 hours in the car if we don't dilly dally around. That will be a long day, but it is along the famous "Garden Route", which is supposed to be beautiful and the reason we are going to Plettenberg Bay. So, we should enjoy it.

I was going to get on the computer, but it is just too nice out here on the porch at the moment. I wish this hotel had a laptop like the Victoria & Albert did. I could sit out here and enjoy the evening while using it. When Linda checked out of the Victoria & Albert she discovered that the laptop wasn't free after all; not only was it not free, it wasn't cheap! Linda explained to the hotel staff, tongue-in-cheek, that had we understood that it was costing us we wouldn't have asked it to join us for drinks! That laptop had two or three great "happy hours"!

I called my mother around 6:30 p.m. (9:30 a.m. her time), but got her answering machine. I left her a message but her not answering worried me a little. She could have just been in the shower, but I would rather have heard her voice. I thought of calling Jaret, but he would have been at work. I picked up my voice mail messages and since there was one my business partner, Dennis, needed to hear, I called and got through to him. We had a good, but short, talk. Man, I am lucky to have that guy in my life! He confirmed what Britt had said that he and others didn't get my last group email.

All that prompted me to go use the hotel's computer (free, I think!). I checked my office emails, re-sent the missing email and wrote a quick update to everyone:

FRANSCHHOEK, SOUTH AFRICA
Subject: South Africa's Wine Country

Hi everyone!

We arrived yesterday (Sunday) in Franschhoek (means French Corner), about 45 minutes east of Cape Town. It is in the heart of South Africa's wine country. And beautiful it is! They sure know how to make rock mountains here. Franschhoek is nestled in a horse shoe of towering rock edifices and the valley floor is matted with vineyards and grand wineries. Truly incredible.

I know, I know. The Seattle weather has been gorgeous. But just so you know we are keeping up, this area is having unseasonably great weather. Not sure what the temp has been, but near 80 with no wind. It did rain last night....and may again tonight....but hey, I am sleeping then, so who cares?

Since you all have been following the saga, I am sure you are wondering what has come of Linda's missing bag. Well, as of today, we hear that it is supposed to be shipped to us in Johannesburg in three days--the day before we leave for our two-week safari trip. She has already done her "replacement shopping" (that's a scary phrase coming from Linda), but she was very happy to hear she will get her clothes. I am a little skeptical; I really hope she isn't disappointed. If there is any good news from this missing bag, it could be that Linda is learning how little she can get by with when travelling! Truly, she has been a champ; she will have been without her suitcase for nine days by the time she gets it back!

Tomorrow, Tuesday, we have an 8-hour drive over the mountains, to the coast and then along the "Garden Route" to a place called Plettenberg Bay. It will be a long day in the car, but the scenery is supposed to be nice. I won't see any of it, because Linda will be after me every time I take my eyes off the road. But I have gotten pretty good at sneaking peeks, so I suspect I will get my share.

Everything is good here....we hope it is with all of you, too.

Gary

TUESDAY, MAY 20

The infinity pool at The Plettenberg Hotel overlooking the Indian Ocean

Today is a gloomy day here in Franschhoek. Low overcast. It is not raining and I don't think it did last night. It is 8 a.m.; the roosters woke me up at 7:15 with the sunrise, which is good. We want a fairly early start on our 7-8 hour drive today. I actually think it will be more like 9 hours because we would like to take in some sights along the way. Nothing specific, just things that look interesting and to give us breaks from the car. Road construction could be a wild card, too.

Last night Linda and I sat on the porch enjoying the gorgeous evening at the end of what had been a gorgeous day and playing gin (I am now up 147, for the record).

For dinner, Linda and I had decided to go to Le Quartier Francais, which is a fine dining bistro with cottages for rent in the heart of the village. I asked Dennis to remind where he and Susan stayed when they were here a few months ago and he said it was Le Quartier Francais, a Relais & Chateaux property. I didn't make the connection on the phone with him last night but did when I was checking my emails. So, I wrote and told him we were going to eat at the place he had stayed. The bistro (and the Inn, although we couldn't see much of it) had the nicest feel to it. Linda and I sat outside by a fireplace and had a great meal and some pretty good South African wine from a winery about ¼ mile up the road from our hotel. (Oops, time for a new pen!)

At the table next to us was a thirty-ish couple form Britain; he was from London, she from Ireland. He had been working in Cape Town the past two weeks on a project requiring his environmental science skills, and she, coincidentally, was on an assignment at the same time in Cape Town, too. She also is a scientist working on a tuberculosis project. She gave me some sobering (frightening) statistics about the extent of the HIV and TB problems in Cape Town alone: 500,000 are infected with HIV, 1,500 get treated for TB every day compared to 1,500 a year in all of England.

They are a young, attractive bright couple who have been married six months and who have traveled extensively. In Australia (where he had worked for three years), New Zealand, Vietnam, Russia and most recently, Ethiopia. She loved Ethiopia and encouraged me to check into it as a destination for ourselves. They are prepared for, and used to, more rugged travel than Linda and me, but I will look into it. They just booked flights to Sierra Leone in December. I was surprised when he said he couldn't find any guidebooks for the country; surprised there were no books and surprised he was concerned. I guess there is a limit to their travel bravado!

While at the Le Quartier Francais restaurant, I broke away to call my mother again since I was worried about not getting through to her earlier. This time I got through; she had, indeed, been in the shower when I called and left a message the first time. She had already called Sheila and Connie to tell them she had missed my call. She sounded good on the phone. She complained that that "damn Connie" is pushing her to do more---that was music to my ears; Mom, is getting back to her old self!

— — —

It is 6 p.m. and I just pulled myself up to the bar at The Plettenberg, our hotel overlooking the Indian Ocean from the hillside in Plettenberg Bay, South Africa. The weather

is marginal, spitting rain, overcast; it was pretty much that way all day today, but at least the visibility was always good.

We rolled into Plettenberg Bay at around 3:30 p.m., only 6½ hours after leaving Franschhoek. The roads were very good; most of them posted with 120 km/hr speed limits versus the 100 km/hr I was expecting. And there were no unexpected construction delays and there were passing lanes on every hill to avoid slow trucks. We zoomed right along. We stopped for gas and potty breaks a couple of times and for an hour-long lunch in Mossel Bay. I was a little weary when we got to Plettenberg Bay, but not bad. It was a much easier day than I expected.

Drivers here are sane. Even more than that, they are courteous and cautious. The roadside service station/deli/diners are amazingly clean. Some of the bathrooms were worthy of hanging out in---if you were so inclined.

The terrain varied dramatically during the journey. We went from the vineyards of Franschhoek to thousands of acres of grain land all of which was fallow so it was brown for as far as one could see across rolling hills; it was pretty. And then we saw orchards of various (unknown to me) kinds. And we saw thousands of sheep; then thousands of cows; and then hundreds of ostriches! A lot

of variety in one day. Linda pointed out how few farm houses we saw. Curious, indeed. I am not sure why that would be.

Having said all of that, I am not sure what all the excitement is over the "Garden Route". For sure, it is nice and it is pretty, but I am not sure it deserves all its acclaim.

When we got to The Plettenberg (another Relais & Chateaux property) we looked out our hotel room window which looks out over the Indian Ocean and saw a pod (school? herd? bunch?) of dolphins just yards off the shore playing in the surf. They weren't far away and looked huge, larger than dolphins I am used to.

This hotel is a very, very nice place. It is perched on a point a hundred feet or so above the water. It has a café and bar overlooking the infinity pool with a grand view out to the ocean. Too bad we are here for only two nights!

After checking out our hotel, we hopped back into the car and drove a few blocks to the main part of town to walk Plettenberg Bay's streets and check out restaurants recommended to us by the hotel staff. We checked out four or five and on the last one Linda looked at me in a panic and said, "Where's my purse!?" How would I know? I am thinking. Well, that and a few other grim thoughts. Before I could finish those thoughts she had already started running down the street frantically checking places we had just been. I hang back near our parked car wondering why she hasn't taken a moment to think about where she might have left it. Having no luck at the first two restaurants, her frenzy now nearing maximum output, she zoomed past me and our car to her third restaurant. Casually, I peered into our parked car to confirm my suspicion; her purse was sitting on the car seat. Too late to stop her from barreling into restaurant number three, I waited until she returned and calmly handed her purse to her.

Part of my distraction (and lack of attention) during Linda's alarm over her lost purse was some commotion nearby down the street from me. Even as small as Plettenberg Bay is, like Cape Town it has parking attendants roaming the streets. Two of them were fighting, fist fighting, in the street apparently over which of them was entitled to some money. I watched to make sure they weren't any immediate threat to Linda or me, but they weren't, and since neither was that accomplished at fighting, I lost interest---which is about the time I looked into our car to spot Linda's "missing" purse.

I am not sure I understand the parking attendant concept. As I have said, Cape Town, Plettenberg Bay and other cities employ uniformed attendants to help you park your car on the streets. Parking here is no different than in the U.S. (except you are doing if from the wrong side of the car), so assistance isn't really required. It could be for added security, but they are generally working on crowded streets, not a likely scenario for vandalism or car theft. Perhaps the cities hire them to help with the 25% unemployment rate. I don't know. Maybe I will have to ask some questions.

After the fight between the two black, male parking attendants was broken up, a white man, who appeared as though he might have been their supervisor, was scolding them. He finished by saying, "Aren't you both South Africans?" When they replied that they were, he said, "Why then are you fighting amongst yourselves, for fuck sake!?" My buddy Murray couldn't have said it better.

The actual undercurrent of this little street conflict and the supervisor's question is likely xenophobic. Currently, there is great pressure, and many killings, in Johannesburg due to the influx of Zimbabweans fleeing their country, its dictator, Robert Mugabe, and its horrible economic conditions for the not-much-better economic opportunities in South Africa. South African's have little sympathy for the fleeing Zimbabweans and do not much appreciate them taking what few jobs there are away. That is why the supervisor asked his question.

The racism in this country, as in ours, is both overt and subtle. I don't know what to think of the riots currently going on in Johannesburg's townships, but it does give me pause about visiting Soweto, the world's largest "ghetto", while we are in Johannesburg. We have planned on it, but we will see how tensions are when we are there.

WEDNESDAY, MAY 21

Linda at Monkeyland near Plettenberg Bay on the phone with British Air

Happy Anniversary Chuck & Kerry. It was Mike Sweeney's birthday on the 15th, I think. We celebrated his and Angela's (May 11) birthdays on the Sunday before we left Seattle.

It is a beautiful morning. I am squinting in the bright sunlight as I sit at The Plettenberg's breakfast table next to the vanishing pool overlooking the ocean. There is no wind and it must be in the mid-70's, or warmer here in the sun. A pretty raucous storm blew through last night, wind and pounding rain, but clearly that has blown on by.

I got up before 7 a.m., walked around, took some photos and then wrote an email home. I got here to the breakfast table around 8:30 a.m. Here is the email I sent home:

PLETTENBERG BAY, SOUTH AFRICA
Subject: Storks or Llamas?

Hello from Plettenberg Bay!

Yesterday afternoon (Tuesday), we arrived at Plettenberg Bay, a six-and-a-half hour leisurely car drive from the wine-lands of Franschhoek. It is now 7:00 am on Wednesday and I am writing from The Plettenberg, our hotel.

Getting here we drove through much of South Africa's famous "Garden Route"; pretty enough but not sure it is deserving of all the acclaim it gets. Leaving the beautiful wine valley of Franschhoek we drove through some fairly desolate, but scenic, countryside as we made our way through the craggy mountains. The valley on the other side was planted mostly in fruit trees and then another valley (an hour) later we were in rolling hills of grain farms. As far as the eye could see, acres and acres of fallow farmland. It is amazing how pretty brown dirt can be. It was at this point we started seeing sheep, thousands and thousands grazing on what little foliage was growing on the fallow land. Sheep lands gave way to cattle country and then to some other less common herds.

As we drive along, I (for the most part) try to watch the road and prompt Linda to check out things I may see but can't focus on.

Suddenly, she blurts out, "Oh my God, look at those, they look like storks or llamas!" Storks or llamas? Hmmmm.... Well, let's first do a leg inventory to narrow it down a bit. Storks or llamas? I mean, even "ostriches or elands" would have made more sense. Too funny. It turns out what she saw were, in fact, probably a group (herd?) of ostriches....lots of ostrich meat in South Africa. Some of you may remember Linda having reported spying some (feathered) "peasants" on a drive through Portugal. Only Linda!

Plettenberg Bay is very pretty. This area is popular with South Africans for their summer vacations. It is very quiet here now, definitely their slow season. Perched on a cliff overlooking the bay and the Indian Ocean our hotel is perfectly located. When we were being shown to our rooms we saw a school (pod? herd? bunch of?) of dolphins merely yards off shore playing in the surf. Whale and dolphin watching are big activities here. So is shark diving...as in Great White Sharks. Not today, thank you.

The weather was pretty much high overcast much of the day yesterday and it spit rain on a few occasions, but it is warm....60's and 70's. We had a storm blow through last night but it looks to be a pretty day today.

I know some of you have read about the "xenophobic" violence, mostly in Johannesburg. It seems this is mostly poor South Africans showing their outrage at Zimbabwean immigrants who have come to South Africa to make a living since their own country is so screwed up. The local papers are indicating this is more likely organized violence from South African business people paying others to intimidate, or worse, their Zimbabwean competitors. I am not sure how it washes out, and don't expect to be effected by it. We only have a short time in Johannesburg and are re-thinking our interest in visiting a Township. Townships are the areas black South Africans were relegated to during the height of Apartheid (70's) and it is in one or two of the larger, poorer ones in Johannesburg where the violence is occurring. Don't worry, Mom, I will stay out of trouble!

I am used to greeting and signing off in the local language (you know, showing off the two words I have learned). Afrikaans is the Dutch-derivative language of South Africa, but it was the language of Apartheid, so I am not thinking it is politically correct to use it....or not sure when it is politically incorrect to use it. Zulu and Xhosa are common tribal languages but you never know who speaks which....and there are a dozen other tribal languages commonly used. So English it is.

Good bye!

Gary

We left the hotel around 7:30 p.m. last night to go to an Asian fusion restaurant that has a great bar overlooking the little town of Plettenberg Bay and the ocean. As usual, we had a good time with the bar tenders and wait staff and had a pretty good Asian dinner. It was a nice evening after a long day. We got back to our room around 10:30 p.m. I slept well; Linda is saying she didn't so much. The bed is very comfy, though.

— — —

The weather turned out great today. It must have been near 80 degrees. It's now about 6 p.m. and I am sitting in The Plettenberg's bar overlooking the ocean. Beautiful.

Linda and I left the hotel this morning at 9:30 and went into The Crags about 20 kilometers east of Plettenberg Bay. No one can explain why it is called The Crags, but it is where Monkeyland and Birds of Eden are.

Monkeyland is a thirty-acre sanctuary for orphaned or previously tamed monkeys; the goal of the sanctuary is to get these monkeys back into the wild at some point. While

there, I think we saw six or seven different species of monkeys and a Malaysian Ape. It was kind of a cool place, actually. It took an hour and had the required guide for a group of eight visitors at a time. I took a bunch of pictures, mostly for practice so I will be ready for our safaris. The practice was needed, I found. In the activity of monkeys jumping all over and coming right up to us, I failed to notice the dial on my Canon Rebel camera got moved from "Av" to "M" and it messed up the exposure for the last bunch of photos. This is okay really; it just made deleting them easier. I deleted most of the properly exposed ones, too. Way too many pictures of monkeys!

Almost as an afterthought, we also went to the Birds of Eden bird sanctuary. It shares a parking lot with Monkeyland and was right next door. The sanctuary is a two-acre enclosed area, enclosed with netting, not a roof. It is actually very well done and we had fun spotting the various species of birds. We saw some incredible colors and plumes on some amazing birds.

You are not supposed to feed or touch the birds, of course, but at one point a little dove-like bird started attacking Linda's feet. I told her we must be close to its nest; he was protecting it. As she walked past that area, it was my turn to pass by and sure enough the little bastard comes after me. I stop and let him attack my shoes which he does with great fervor. I was in the process of struggling to get one of my cameras in position to take a photo of him when he suddenly flies from my feet to the top of my head! It was about that time I got my small camera set to take video, so I aimed it at me and my head. What resulted is a pretty funny video of the little bird flying back and forth between the top of my head and my hand holding the camera. After a while of playing with him, I reached my

hand to a nearby handrail so he could jump off. We walked on leaving our little buddy to his next victim.

Not much later, I encounter a parrot sitting on a ledge very near our walkway. As I ease around him, he makes it clear he doesn't like me that close to him. I know parrots can be pretty persnickety and ornery so I respectfully give him plenty of room. Safely past him ten yards I hear fluttering and then feel a bird land on my head. A gray bird with a brightly colored red tail had flown out of nowhere and took my head for a perch. I am starting to get a complex about my head! But before I have time to think much about that, the parrot I had just irritated flies over and lands on my shoulder! I am a little befuddled because with a bird on my head and one on my shoulder, everything is so close to me I can't quite get what is going on.

When Red Tail sees Parrot Bird encroaching on his prize, he drops down to my shoulder and attacks Parrot Bird. So, here I am the battle ground for this bird argument and I am trying to hand the camera to Linda so she can film it. These are reasonably good sized birds and they are making lots of noise. Linda is laughing, but she is also intimidated and is afraid to get too close. Finally, the birds come to some sort of truce, apparently deciding I am big enough to share, so Red Tail moves over to my other shoulder. Turning my head from side to side to look at the birds on my shoulders, I see each bird is craning his neck to see around my face to glare at the other. Apparently, it was an uneasy truce. As I am doing this, the glitter of my teeth catches their attention. This caused them to lose interest in each other and to move in and start pecking at my teeth! Caught off

guard I quickly I close my lips. They are persistent. They have seen those pearly whites and they want some of that. They are actually being surprisingly gentle and aren't hurting me (although later I would see that I ended up with several bright red spots on my lower lip.) Soon, my two antagonists settle down and, perhaps feeling guilty for involving me in their dispute, start nuzzling me with their heads and preening my hair. A sudden loud squawk in my left ear from Red Tail made me jump, sending them both off to fight other battles.

So much for not touching the birds!

From The Crags we drove down to the beach at nature's Valley, took a few pictures of a very pretty, isolated and vacant beach, and then drove back to Plettenberg Bay for lunch. In the meantime, using her cell phone, Linda had been making a series of phone calls and learned that our hotel in Johannesburg has received her luggage and it will be there waiting for her when we arrive tomorrow night. Great news.

We got back to our hotel, The Plettenberg, at around three in the afternoon. We went outside and laid on lawn chairs in the grass next to the pool. Laying there in 80 degree windless weather overlooking the Indian Ocean---what a glorious day!

We read and hung out there until 4:30ish. I showered and took a drive to take some sunset photos from a place I had spotted earlier. I came back to the hotel's bar, deleted a bunch of the pictures I had taken today and then caught up in my journal---and here I am.

It is now 7:30 p.m. and it is time to move on to some dinner.

THURSDAY, MAY 22

Sunrise from The Plettenberg Hotel

What a pretty sunrise! It is 7 a.m. and I am sitting on the terrace overlooking the Indian Ocean at The Plettenberg Hotel. I am at the hotel's breakfast café having coffee. The light blue sky and the scattered high cirrus clouds are reflecting off the pool water. The clouds are pink from the yet-to-rise sun and the ocean's water is slate-colored. The backdrop is the silhouette of the Tsitsikamma Mountains. Wow. So far, I have to say, South Africa has been beautiful everywhere we have been.

The hotel has two black cats; Oliver and Peter. Pretty cool cats. A little haughty, self-absorbed and spoiled, but then, they are cats. They are also friendly and cute as hell. Peter is drinking out of the pool at the moment and his black frame is silhouetted against the oceanic scene I just described. A seagull, a beautiful black-tip winged gull, made an aerial approach to land on the pool's infinity edge, but did a go-around instead apparently deciding not to tempt Peter. When I was signing the hotel's guest register last night, Oliver jumped right onto the book and plopped down---I had to move his butt over to finish signing.

We left the hotel in our car last night about 7:30 headed downtown to eat. We stopped in at Miguel's before going to our dinner location because the bar looked fun. Somehow it looked fun, even though it was empty at the time. This whole town, the whole area, is empty. Major off-season. At Miguel's Linda started her process of asking a million questions about the menu, even though we didn't plan on eating there. I didn't mind because the two hostesses Linda was pestering with questions were way cute. We were sitting at the bar with our glasses of wine. Not surprisingly, something sounded good to Linda so we decided to eat there, right there at the bar. Perfect for me. The cute hostess suggested a chicken dish that came on a vertical skewer; it was way good.

Damn, did I mention how gorgeous it is sitting here? As the sun comes up, the picture changes, seemingly getting more and more dramatic. Sitting here alone with my steaming cup of coffee half way around the world from home. I've got the sunrise, Peter, Oliver and a black-tip winged gull---life is grand! Rats, here comes Linda. Solitude over!

The Champions Game, the World Cup of European soccer, was being played and shown on the TV at Miguel's last night. The game was being played in Moscow between Chelsea and Manchester United, two English teams. I think the announcer said it was the first time ever.

Everyone, which means Miguel's employees since Linda and I were the only customers, was rooting for Man U. If we would have had SIM card time left, I would have called Murray who I am sure took the day off in Seattle to watch the match, even though his team, Arsenal, wasn't playing. It was tied at one at half time and was still tied when we left before the game was over. We were in bed by 11 p.m.

Our wake-up call was at 6:15 this morning. We drive to Port Elizabeth this morning, which will take about 2½ hours, to catch a 12:35 p.m. flight to Johannesburg. One night at the Peech Hotel in Johannesburg where Linda's luggage is supposed to be waiting for her and then off to the Okavango Delta!

FRIDAY, MAY 23

Our first sunset in Botswana near Chief's Camp

We are sitting at the Johannesburg airport awaiting our departure to Maun, Botswana. It is 9:30 a.m. Let me catch up with yesterday's events after leaving Plettenberg Bay.

Our drive to Port Elizabeth yesterday was easy. It took about 2½ hours even with a couple of delays and detours for road construction. It was a pretty drive, but like the rest of the Garden Route, nothing outstanding. We drove around Port Elizabeth a little, to see the beaches mostly, filled the rental car with gas and bought some batteries. We then turned the car back into Avis. We had driven a total of 1,400 kilometers (850 miles) since picking the car up at the Cape Town airport nine days ago.

At the Port Elizabeth airport, I talked to a group of South African women who were part of a net ball team. Net ball is a game like basketball without dribbling; I understand it is played mostly by women and is relatively common in the Commonwealth countries (net ball was begun in England in the 1890's). A couple of the girls (the two black girls) were pretty darned sexy, which of course, is why I started talking to them in the first place. They were very curious about Linda and me: where we were from, what kind of work we did, etc. I have never seen a net ball game before; I will have to try to catch one on TV or something.

We just boarded our plane to Maun.

Our flight yesterday landed in Johannesburg on time. We had a 45-minute taxi ride from the Johannesburg airport to The Peech Hotel where we stayed last night. The Peech is a small, quaint, nice hotel in Johannesburg's Melrose district.

When we arrived at the Peech Hotel in Johannesburg in the early evening, the first thing Linda saw in the lobby of the small hotel was her missing bag. British Airlines had finally gotten it delivered it to her after taking nine days to find it. She ran up to it and hugged and kissed it like it has a newly found lost child. I was happy for her.

After checking in, we both took time to re-pack our bags for the last portion—the safari portion--of our trip. Limited to 40 pounds a person because of the small airplanes used to get to, and between, the camps, we planned on leaving the "extra" stuff in a bag at the Peech Hotel where we will pick it up two weeks later when we pass back through on our way home.

It was about 5 p.m. by the time I got down to The Peech's bar last night. The hotel was setting up for a wine dinner put on by a Stellenbosch winery. We got invited, so we stayed and took part in what turned out to be a great dinner with good wine.

During the wine dinner, we sat next to two white South Africans, Nick and Le Marie, who lived in Johannesburg, not far from the Peech Hotel. They spoke very matter-of-factly about violence in Johannesburg. Most residential communities are built behind security fences or walls and most houses have protective razor wire. Self-policing is normal in most communities because the police can't keep up with the crime; in their neighborhood, residents take turns patrolling the perimeter of their neighborhoods. After talking about this for many minutes, Le Marie casually mentions, almost as an afterthought, that Nick had gotten shot! It was a horrifying story, but one they insist is not that uncommon. Nick had pulled into their driveway to their garage door in their "protected" neighborhood and got shot sitting at the wheel of his car with their two small girls in the back seat. The shot was meant for his head, but the bullet grazed his chin and went through his bicep. The true horror of this conversation is how this level of crime is considered unremarkable in Johannesburg. Linda and I were glad to be heading out to the bush where all we had to worry about were marauding elephants, man-eating lions and killer hippos!

I am going to take a break and watch the scenery out the plane's window.

— — —

We saw lions on our first game drive! It's about 6 p.m. and I am sitting in our tent at Chief's Camp after a great afternoon. Time to catch up.

It was a 1½ hour flight from Johannesburg to

Maun. It was a pretty simple matter of getting our luggage at the Maun airport and connecting to our Mack Air flight for our short flight to Chief's Camp. The Mack Air plane was a ten-seat, single engine turbo prop, much like the planes we flew in Belize. We were only in the air for about ten minutes before landing on a dirt strip to drop some folks off at Baines Camp. We took off again in minutes and flew another five minutes to another camp where more folks deplaned and who appeared to be a couple of camp employees boarded. We then flew the final ten minutes to Chief's camp. Each of the land strips were hard-packed dirt cleared of brush.

While flying in Mack Air we flew at about 500 feet above the absolutely flat terrain. It made for great sightseeing. We were spotting impalas, elephants and giraffes. Linda thought she saw either a stork or a llama—this time it ended up being a Wildebeest.

We were flying into the Okavango Delta which is a huge inland delta formed where the Okavango River reaches a huge bowl (tectonic trough) in the Kalahari Desert covering most of northwestern Botswana. Maun is at the southeastern edge of the Okavango Delta and acts as the main entry point. All the water reaching the Okavango Delta is ultimately evaporated or soaked into the ground and does not flow into any sea or ocean. The Okavango River drains the summer (January–February) rainfall from the Angola highlands and the waters then spread over the Delta over the next four months (March–June). The flood peaks between June and August, during Botswana's dry winter months, when the Okavango swells to three times its permanent size, attracting animals from miles around and creating one of Africa's greatest concentrations of wildlife. We were arriving in the Okavango Delta as the water was rising and the climate was moderate; a great time to visit.

We learned before we arrived some of the details of safari operations in Botswana. Botswana grants either licenses or concessions to private operators for the purpose of conducting safaris. There are many restrictions, most of which are intended to protect the animals and their habitat. This is why the safari camps are all temporary; built just for the season, they cannot have foundations. Accordingly, all of the "rooms" and buildings at the camps are tents. The "room" tents are, by the way, embarrassingly nice, including hardwood floors, complete bathrooms and super nice bed linens. The operators are also required to hire people from Botswana, in particular, the guides. In exchange for all of this (and probably a pretty healthy stipend), the camp operators are allowed semi-exclusive access to a national reserve, or in the case of a concession, exclusive use to a very large area. The advantage of this is that you don't normally see another vehicle, and if you do, it is from your camp.

An important rule in safari camp life is that you never walk around after dark without being accompanied by a guide; not even if your tent is a mere twenty yards from the main tent. We have heard chilling stories about those who didn't heed that warning. I didn't come to Africa to be dinner.

From the Chief's Camp landing strip, we had a seven minute jeep ride to Chief's Camp in the Okavango Delta in Botswana. During that short ride, we saw several bunches of impala and an elephant. This was exciting; this was going to be fun!

The setting of Chief's Camp is gorgeous; has a 24-person capacity, but only 22 are here. When we arrived they greeted us with cool, wet washcloths and cold drinks (non-alcoholic). They then served lunch to the four of us who arrived together, which was much needed; it was 2:30 p.m. and Linda and I last ate at 6:30 a.m. I guess I have missed the part where we started this day with a 5:30 a.m. wake-up call.

After lunch, we started our first game drive. We left the camp at 3:30 p.m. in a "landie". "Landie" is the local nickname which conveniently encompasses both the Land Rovers and Land Cruisers that are invariably used for safaris. There were six people in our landie with Jonathan, our guide/driver.

Impala are as numerous as trees here, we saw lots of them. We saw some kudu (I told you we would see real live ones after eating them in Cape Town!), zebra, elephants, giraffes, wart hogs---all in their natural and amazing settings. This really is Africa.

Another landie had spotted some lions, so our landie joined them to watch the lions. One lion was carrying in his mouth the hindquarter of a small giraffe, what was left of his dinner apparently.

We watched them for forty-five minutes or so until they walked over to a watering hole. We watched as the two lions knelt at water's edge lapping water as the sun set. My photos should be amazing. They drank forever. I don't know how much they get with each lap, but they slurped noisily for twenty minutes.

Both the elephants and the lions, at various times, were within twenty feet of our landie---much to Linda' dismay. She was very anxious. I am sure she will get a little more used to it. One of the elephants got a little upset and aggressive with us, which really got Linda going.

Right now, 7:30 p.m., Jonathan is really pissing us off. We are in our cabin and cannot leave it after dark without a guide to escort us. So, they arrange for us to make an appointment to come escort you to the lodge at the appointed time. Ours was for 6:45 p.m., 45 minutes ago. We are stuck here with no way to communicate; nothing we can do but sit and wait. There is an emergency horn you can blare for emergencies, which hardly seems appropriate---or does it? This could have a significant effect on his tip!

SUNDAY, MAY 25

Our tent's porch at Chief's Camp in Botswana

It is noon and I am sitting in a luxuriously comfortable lounge chair on our cabin's porch overlooking the marshland in front of Chief's Camp. Both yesterday and this morning they woke us up at 6 a.m. and fed us at 6:30 a.m.; we were in the landie at 7 a.m. They provide us with insulated ponchos and warm water bottles when we get into the landies; they are needed, it is pretty cool that time in the morning, and after the sun sets.

We have the same six people (including Linda and me) and the same guide each time we go out for a game drive and the seven of us eat our meals together. In our landie we have Bill and Leann from Boulder, Colorado and Jeff and Isla from Canberra, Australia. Everyone is nice and fun to be with. Our guide, Jonathan, is a spitting image of our Seattle friend, Celester.

Yesterday morning's drive lasted until 12:30 p.m. and today's, only until 11:00 a.m. Each afternoon drive started at 3:30 p.m. and ended at dark, around 6:30 p.m. This morning's drive was the fourth one so far and was the only time we didn't see something new or exciting.

I described the two lions we saw on our first drive two days ago as the sun was setting. Yesterday morning, I spotted a lion which ended up being a female in a pride of lions; the dominant male, two cubs and four or so females. We watched them moving around for an hour. It was way cool. I am credited and heralded as "eagle eye" for spotting the lion.

Then on yesterday afternoon's game drive we heard very loud elephant trumpeting and crashing. As loud as it was, you could tell the source of the noise was still a kilometer or so away. Jonathan, drove the landie cautiously toward the racket to investigate. He was being very careful; we had learned that locals fear nothing more in the wild than a charging elephant.

As we neared the raucous noise, even though nothing was yet visible, Jonathan stopped the landie and put it in reverse to get turned around for a quick get-away from what was clearly a very agitated elephant. As we were finishing our turn-around maneuver, an elephant suddenly came crashing through a large Acacia tree headed right for us from only forty yards away. Emerging through the dust raised from thrashing and crashing through trees, the dark figure of this huge animal rushed toward us like a cyclone. Tusks and a waving trunk became visible; the intensity of trumpeting was shocking.

I was happy to see Jonathan, maneuvering with great earnestness to get the landie moving away from this looming threat. But when the elephant became fully visible to Jonathon, he visibly relaxed. It was a young elephant bull and, by elephant standards, not that large. In Jonathan's mind we were witnessing a teenage fit, not a serious and dangerous charge from a mature bull. The young bull stopped not far from our landie, swinging his large head back and forth, flapping his ears and trumpeting to warn us away. We did move away, but we continued to follow the agitated, young bull from a safe distance looking for the leopard or lion which may have set him off, but we never saw anything. The young bull continued his tirade, inexplicably, for quite a while. Jonathan joked that maybe the elephant had a toothache. As agitated as he was, I told Jonathan it had to be something more serious, like elephant hemorrhoids.

After that we got a radio call from another of our camp's landies and we went to see the leopard the other landie had spotted. They were about a mile away. The leopard was amazing; a sleek, lithe, beautiful cat. We watched as the leopard eyed the zebras and impalas that were grazing the meadow not far away. We left him at dark. He probably ate about the same time we did two hours later.

When we got back to Chief's Camp about 6:45 p.m., it marked the end of our first full day in the Okavango. I went to our cabin and used the outdoor shower. I got escorted by Jonathan (this time as scheduled at 7:15 p.m.) to the lodge so that I could write a group email home using their computer:

CHIEF'S CAMP, BOTSWANA
Subject: Wild Kingdom...up close and personal

Hi everyone,

I only have moments.

We just finished our first complete day at Chief's Camp in the Okavango Delta in Botswana. We have had three game drives. Dennis told me exactly what to expect and that I would really like it. And of course he was spot on. But he didn't, because no one can, describe how truly incredible it is to be in the wilderness within feet of amazing animals; many of which you don't want to make mad. I won't--can't--bore you now with all that we have seen.....but I will when I get home!!

We are having a great time....we have all of our clothes and they are enough to keep us warm...and cool. The accommodations are embarrassingly nice and the guides knowledgeable and friendly. It is all good.

Another day here and then we move south to Baines Camp. I will try to write again, but frankly, there isn't much time to do so....and there are others wanting to write home waiting behind me.

I will talk to you soon.

Gary

Dinners both nights have been (and will be) barbeques on the sand boma. Bomas are the enclosures of fences made of thorn bushes to protect against animals. The dining tables at Chief's Camp are set up on the sand surface outside the lodge under the stars with the marsh right next to us. While dining and conversing with other campers about the day's exciting sightings and events, the crickets and frogs make a cacophony of jungle music and fruit bats circle overhead. The southern hemisphere night sky shines brilliantly overhead. I have had barbeque Kudu and crocodile and some "mystery meat stew". The food has been amazing, but the dining setting is out of this world.

I will be surprised if Linda goes out on this afternoon's game drive. If not, it will be just Jonathan and me in the landie. Maybe we will see the White Rhinoceros we looked for this morning, but I doubt we will; they range quite a ways away from our camp and there is less time in the afternoon drive to get to that area and back. Whatever we do, and see, will be great.

One thing I have failed to mention is the traditional morning tea. Around 10 a.m. Jonathan stops the landie pulls out a small table, hot water and biscotti, or something similar. I always know when he is about to do this because he drives in circles around his intended stopping place, checking to be sure we don't pull up and stop unwittingly next to a sleeping lion, or some other lurking danger. He will also select a place near a termite mound that we all can use as a screen for a potty break. I also notice how watchful Jonathan is during these breaks; outside the landie we are fair game. A reminder we are in the wild.

By mentioning just the highlights of the game drives so far, I have given no credit to the constant game sightings. There are impalas at every turn. Elephants, zebras,

giraffes, wildebeests, kudu and warthogs are literally everywhere. We have seen the occasional mongoose and steenbok (an antelope about the size of a large cat). Baboons and vervets are all around the camp. And birds, amazingly colorful and pretty---too numerous to mention.

Time to get ready for the afternoon drive.

— — —

It is 7 p.m. I am waiting in my Chief's Camp cabin for Jonathan to escort me.

It was, indeed, only Jonathan and me on this afternoon's game drive.

He and I went looking for cheetah, with no luck. But that search did take us to the "plains" area. On this 40 by 25 mile island that we are on, it is amazing how much, yet how little, the terrain varies. It is flat everywhere and there isn't a rock of any size on the whole island. But the flora changes dramatically over fairly short distances.

As the sun was setting, Jonathan pulled over near the edge of a large, grassy plain to have our "sundowner"---my first of the trip. This is the afternoon version of the morning tea tradition. I love the morning teas, but the concept of having a drink to watch the sun set in the middle of the wild is right down my alley. It was magical. While I sipped my gin and tonic next to a little table Jonathan and I had set up, he and I talked about family, Americans and his personal desire to move on and do something different. As we talked and gazed out over the plain in front of us, we could see a small herd of elephants off in the distance. Giraffes were loping across the grassy field and feeding on some trees around its edge. Above, two Sea Eagles circled, eyeing the Guinea Fowl we could see rushing through a bare spot in the ground to the cover of the tall grasses. The sounds of unseen animals, insects and birds were background to our soft conversation. Like I said. It was magical.

MONDAY, MAY 26

The pool at Baines Camp

It is 1:00 p.m. and I am sitting next to the little pool at Baines Camp in the Okavango delta. We arrived here from Chief's Camp around noon after a 15-minute flight and an hour drive from the landing strip. After arriving, we had some lunch, watched hippos in the water in front of the camp's lodge and got checked into our cabin. I am now lounging as we wait for our afternoon drive to start, our first at Baines Camp. This camp is more rustic than Chief's Camp, and very cool.

It was just Linda and me for this morning's last game drive from Chief's Camp. We threw our bags into the landie when we left the camp, so we could be taken directly to the airstrip at 9:45 a.m. to catch our plane to come here to Baines Camp.

Jonathan has great eyes. During this morning's drive somehow he identified the brown spot in the middle of a plain as a lion. It was a male lion, laid out flat sleeping. We drove right up to it. Without even moving his massive head, he watched our landie pull up to within thirty feet of him. We stopped. He closed his eyes. It was what the "King of the Jungle" does.

Jonathan identified him as the male of the pride I spotted two days earlier. The lion's belly was extended with a recently eaten meal. He seemed to be barely able to breathe (I've been there). Jonathan said he could eat up to 80 pounds in one meal (that I haven't done)! Eventually, the lion slowly got up, sauntered to a nearby watering hole then moved to some shade at the edge of the plain and plopped back down. There were two groups of impalas in different directions only a hundred meters away, watching every move the lion made.

We drove away and onto the main "road" to Maun; eight hours of driving away. This "road" is no more than a track like everything we have driven on, except the track was wider from the larger trucks carrying supplies to Chief's Camp and Mambo Camp, the only two camps on the north half of the island, I think.

As we started heading toward the airstrip to catch our flight to Baines Camp, we spied two giraffes right next to the track. They were lined up, getting ready to mate. The female was backed up to the male, wiggling her haunches, clearly in heat. These two graceful animals stood quietly together waiting for the male's erection. When ready, he lunged up, but missed. There was some post-lunge prancing around, mostly by the frustrated female. Then they resumed their quiet position, her backed up to him, saucily wriggling her hips, encouraging and exciting him. Once ready he would lunge again. We watched three unsuccessful attempts over the course of about 45 minutes before we had to drive away to catch our plane. Jonathan said that in his whole life living in this area, and twenty-plus years of guiding, he had never even heard of anyone ever witnessing what we just had. He said this was when giraffes were at their most vulnerable because it may take them as long as two days to have a successful coupling, and as we saw, both animals are so engrossed they are unaware of their surroundings. It was a remarkable thing to see.

Over the last couple of days at Chief's Camp, Linda had gotten to know Natalie, who was working to get the camp set up for a large, and apparently wealthy, family coming to the camp from around the world for a family gathering. The family members were taking up all of the available units of the camp so Natalie and her crew were setting up tents for the 22 support staff the family hired to take care of them. These staff included such people as cooks, nutritionists, masseuses, doctors, photographers and some others I am forgetting. One I may never forget, though, is the trainer the family brought in, Toni.

Linda and I met Toni and Natalie last night around the boma and had great fun with them. Both are young, attractive, fit women. Toni asked about my exercise regimen; she was impressed, but I joked that since jogging in the African countryside is considered bad for your health, the only exercise I have been getting is keeping myself upright in the bouncing landies. She flirted with me, telling me my trainer at home must love me because I am not only diligent about exercise, but adorable. Aahh, isn't she sweet? And perceptive!? Yeah, Linda didn't' think so either. Like any good wife, she "popped me with a pin" to deflate my ego.

The aggravating part of that story is that we had to leave the camp earlier than normal this morning because the family was arriving. Had that not been the case, we would not have had to cut our morning drive short and could have watched the mating giraffes longer.

When we got to the airstrip, I tipped and thanked

Jonathan (having totally gotten over the first night that he had abandoned us in our cabin!). He was genuinely a good guy. We developed an uncanny friendship during our short time together, much of the bonding occurring during our solo game drive and the conversations we had during our magical sundowner. I will miss him.

I sat in the front right seat of the airplane which was a Cessna 206 (a six-person plane with a piston engine); a plane I have flown several times as the pilot from the left seat. We saw all sorts of giraffes and elephants from our 700 foot cruising altitude. When we came in for our landing, a couple of landies (presumably from our camp and possibly another nearby one) were lined up along the dirt landing strip. They do this to chase off any animals that might wander onto the hard-packed dirt air strip.

After we deplaned and loaded into the landie for the hour-long trip to Baines Camp, I spotted a leopard about 75 meters off the track. The driver (who I don't think is a guide, but I don't know yet) drove off the track to where the leopard was. No leopard. It had to be hunched down and hiding behind a small thicket; had we driven around it, I am sure we would have seen our leopard. But the driver says, "I can't imagine where he went, and drove off!" A leopard is a prized sighting, and this guy makes no effort!? I was frustrated. I hope he isn't our guide here at Baines Camp!

WEDNESDAY, MAY 28

Sunset from Boro River near Baines Camp

It is 1:30 p.m. on our second and last full day at Baines Camp. I am now sitting on our cabin's lanai listening to birds and the nearby hippos. The hippos aren't visible to me, but they are probably within 30 to 40 meters. The bush root is hiding them. I haven't written since we first arrived at Baines Camp around noon on Monday; I have some catching up to do.

Here at Baines Camp Kot is our guide and Wanko is the spotter; something we didn't have at Chief's Camp and don't really need here. I concluded Wanka is nothing more than a guide-in-training. Since we are on a concession here at Baines Camp (rather than a reserve as at Chief's Camp), we are able to do night drives. So, at Baines the afternoon drive starts at 4 p.m. (rather than Chief's 3:30 p.m.) and can go until 8 p.m. (rather than Chief's nightfall, or 6:30 p.m.).

Kot, Wanko, Linda and I were joined for Monday's evening drive by Axel and Katrine, a young, professional German couple from Frankfurt. They are mid- to late-thirties and attractive; both tall and slender. He is a partner with Ernst & Young in the management consulting department and she is the investment director for a large mid-cap investment fund. They are smart and Prussian; coolly friendly (at least initially) and they rarely show any signs of affection toward each other. But now, after spending nearly every waking hour with them for two days, they have warmed up to us considerably. We like them.

Our first evening/night drive was so uneventful I can't even think when we had the all-important sundowner or what we saw during the drive. I do recall Kot pointing out the Southern Cross and Orion's Belt and learning how you can tell direction from each of them. I also know we saw nothing significant, or I would remember it.

Before that first night's drive started, we re-connected with Jeff & Isla, Bill & Leann and Carol & Susan from Chief's Camp. We had fun exchanging stories from when we all had last seen each other at Chief's Camp. After that night's evening drive they boasted how they had seen Spotted Hyenas under the spotlight. (As I already pointed out, we saw little, except for the eye reflection of a Bushbaby, a pocket-size monkey). There were two hyena cubs playing near their den, and then their evil-looking parents showed up. It sounded awesome; I was jealous. I have wanted to see hyenas badly.

After that night's drive, everyone sat around the campfire chatting before we sat down to eat. I got to know Carol and Susan (both are from Toronto, Susan is a doctor) well that night and the next morning at breakfast before they had to leave to catch a plane. I liked them a lot.

That night, and again last night, I had my mosquito-net-covered bed pulled out of our cabin onto its lanai so I could sleep under the stars. The lanai is elevated four or five feet from the ground and has a wood rail. The cabins and beds at Baines Camp are set up for this and, to my amazement, I am the only person in the camp taking advantage of it. It is true that we are in the bush, that we can't even leave our cabin at night without a guide because of the danger, and that I suppose I would be an enticing meal to some critters. But, we are sleeping in tents! If some such critter was hungry, he ain't going to let a tent flap stop him! Lying outside in bed I am able to see the incredible night sky, hear hippos moving around, hyenas howling in the distance, and many other things I can't identify. It is very, very cool.

We got up as normal yesterday (Tuesday) and instead of doing a game drive, Axel, Katrine, Linda and I had elected to take in the "Elephant Interaction" with Doug Graves, who it turns out is from Portland, Oregon. Doug runs this enterprise and funds his care for the elephants by charging folks like us to spend a few hours with these huge beasts. Doug adopted two of his three elephants when they were just two years old; Jabu, the male, and Thembi, the female. Since adopting the elephants, Doug has devoted his entire life to living with and caring for these elephants; raising them and caring for them as a parent for the past 24 years. He rescued and adopted the third elephant, Morula, a female, eleven years ago. We all picnicked with the three elephants out in the bush. The lunch was amazingly good. Lots of pictures were taken, most of them set up by Doug, which was just fine.

During the hours we were with him and the elephants, Doug did a great job of educating our group about elephants in general and allowing us intimate and close-up interactions with his three "kids". It had a very little bit of a contrived circus feel to it, but ultimately, it was great fun. Elephants are special creatures.

One of the highlights of this excursion were the daughters of a very nice St. Louis couple, who were staying if a different, nearby camp. Annie was a soccer playing Emery student in her junior year and Liz was a second year medical student. Both were cute, dynamic girls who were not self-possessed and who everyone seemed to enjoy, even the elephants.

We didn't get back to Baines Camp after the Elephant Interaction until almost 2 p.m. Linda went out to lay by the little pool Baines Camp. I relaxed in our cabin and probably napped some. It wasn't long before Linda left the pool to join me; it made her nervous to be at the pool which was elevated four feet or so, but otherwise without any barricade from the wild. I showered, shaved and then went with Linda to the boma for "high tea" at 3:30 p.m.

That afternoon at four, Axel, Katrine, Linda and I hopped into a boat from Baines Camp with Kot and Wanko for a cruise down the Boro River. This river appears to be not much more than a narrow channel through the bush roots with an occasional lagoon. In the first lagoon, we saw a hippo, which means we saw two eyes, a nose and ears. We watched him from a distance for a while, which means three seconds of seeing him for every five minutes of looking for where he would next surface for a breath. Elephants are good swimmers; hippos don't swim, they just walk along under water, apparently.

We saw more hippos, lots of birds and two huge Fish Eagles, which mightily resemble Bald Eagles. The Fish Eagles were sitting side-by-side on a limb eyeing the water for prey. We watched as a vervet monkey scurried out onto the branch to chase away the winged intruders. After doing so, the monkey sat on the limb, strutting and pounding his chest letting the world know that was HIS limb and no one else's.

Being on the water as the sun lowered in the sky was very serene and pleasant. We had a sundowner with the boat nosed into the bush root as an anchor and the absolutely gorgeous sunset behind us.

When we got back to camp right at dark, we four hopped into a landie with Kot and Wanko for a night game drive. Here at Baines Camp they use Toyota's Land Cruiser, at Chief's Camp they used the Range Rover. Specifically, we were going out to see if the hyenas were at their den. Hyenas do move their dens, but we were going to where our friends had seen them the night before in hopes they would still be there. Unless out hunting at night, hyenas will spend most of their time in their dens which are generally underground inside a dead termite mound; the cubs rarely come outside.

We were in luck. When we got to the den, the two cubs were outside the den; one of the adults was there too, but barely visible in the dark so we didn't get a good look at it. The two cubs were curious and exploring. We got great views of them as they would come within ten feet of our landie. It amazes me we can drive right up to them, shine lights in their faces and they don't even seem to notice or react.

When we got back to camp around 7:30 p.m., we met the two newcomers to the camp, Roger and Angela from New York City. They were in their mid-thirties, very nice with great personalities. Bill and Leann went to bed early, so it left Roger, Angela, Alex and Katrine with us around the fire drinking after dinner. Very, very fun. Lots of laughs, especially as Axel and Katrine have loosened up so much.

This morning's drive made up for the dearth of sightings we had previously had here at Baines Camp. Katrine really wanted to see a Wildebeest. I had yet to see an African Buffalo (often mislabeled Water Buffalo and formerly known as Cape Buffalo, I learned). Well, we saw both. So Katrine and I were verbally high-fiving when Kot got a radio call that someone had spotted African Wild Dogs.

African Wild Dogs are a rare sighting because they are constantly on the move and have broad ranges. I had no expectation of seeing one. I was eager to see African Wild Dogs because of a Planet Earth film documentary I saw about them; amazing filmography from the air of a pack of these wild dogs surrounding, attacking and killing its prey. The African Wild Dog is one of the most efficient hunters in the world, credited for being 80% successful in bringing down its prey, which oftentimes,

like a Wildebeest, can be ten times the size of an individual dog. The packs are generally from twenty to forty in number. We were able to locate the pack and spend some time viewing them. Next to the wolf, they are the largest dogs in the world. Seeing them may well be a highlight of the trip.

After that we noted hundreds of vultures circling and perched in trees. We drove to investigate and spotted---smelled---what the attraction was. A full-size giraffe carcass that appeared mostly intact, indicating that neither a predator (lion) nor a scavenger (hyena) had yet been there. After further inspection, we saw that the carcass had been “bored out” through a hole in its soft belly and that the vultures were crawling in and out of the now hollowed-out giraffe body. It had clearly, from appearance and smell, been there a day or two. How had it died? Why had the scavengers not found it? It is all guess work. Possibly the giraffe was killed in a battle over dominance with another giraffe. Or maybe it had died of old age. Anyway, the number of vultures---literally thousands, not hundreds---was awe-inspiring. And it was interesting to watch them fight over the carcass.

We stopped upwind from the carcass for our morning tea and for a break from the god-awful smell. As usual, Kot found an opening in the brush near a termite mound. He got out and walked behind the mound clapping his hands to scare away any lurking critters so we could use that area for our "facilities", which we all took turns doing during our tea break. All done, we hopped back into the landie and drove away. As we did so, we spotted a leopard on the backside of the termite mound peering through the grass not a hundred yards away from where we each had stood/squatted. The leopard had likely watched each of us do our thing; it is surprising he didn't scurry away, but maybe he had initially been much closer. Can't a guy get any privacy around here? We approached him in the landie, but he moved into the trees and we weren't able to spot him again. Twice foiled by leopards at Baines Camp!

FRIDAY, MAY 30

African Buffalo near Baines Camp

I am in our hut at Tongabezi Lodge near Livingstone, Zambia. It is 8 a.m. We have slept in for the first time in a while. I am at a desk in our hut looking out over the Zambezi River from about five feet away and two feet above the water level. There is very little movement of water this close to shore, but the river does move from west to east toward the mighty Victoria Falls about five miles away. It is presently very quiet and serene here; the hippos are across the river right now. More on that later.

I last wrote midday on Wednesday while at Baines Camp. That night's drive was just Axel, Katrine, Linda, me and the guides. We didn't see anything to speak of. Since Kot had to take off for a scheduled medical appointment, we now had Ben with the same spotter, Wanko. As we were returning to camp around 7:30 p.m., Ben leaned out of the landie with the spot light checking tracks. I was right behind him seeing what he was seeing. He proclaimed there were fresh leopard tracks, so fresh he could smell them. After several intense days in the bush, I am actually getting reasonably good at seeing and identifying lion, hyena, leopard and elephant spoor, nothing of course on the level of the guides, but I saw nothing but a tire track when Ben made his proclamation. So, for the next twenty minutes of trying to spot this leopard with a spot light, I am quite dubious. I am convinced Ben was trying to drum up a little excitement when there was none to be had. After a few "possible sightings" with the spot light, Ben shakes his head and pronounces the grass too high this time of year.

I was disappointed that I was so skeptical of Ben and Wanko. I was spoiled by Jonathan at Chief's Camp. I feared my lack of confidence in Ben and Wanko would make the next morning's game drive, may last at Baines, long and uninteresting.

That night, Wednesday, we were joined by Bill and Mary from Washington D.C. She was probably near 60, he maybe ten years older. She was a dynamo, a former stewardess ("yes that is what they called us back when that meant something," she said) who later owned a couple of travel agencies. Single for most of her years, she raised her daughters then married Bill about five years ago. She was, I am sure, a hottie when younger; she was still quite attractive, poised and intelligent. Bill is a complete idiot.

It was only her self-restraint that kept her from slapping him. I was an inch from stuffing his napkin into his mouth, myself. Mary and I were alone for a few minutes by the fire when she confided that he was a big mistake and that they would be divorcing when they got home. I suggested it might be simpler to just give him the boot from the landie the next time they sidle up to a lion.

Linda was beat so she retired from the fire as did Mary and (thank God) Bill. That left me, Axel & Katrine, Roger & Angela and Sean & Elka, the last two being the married couple who manage Baines Camp. Early thirties, the two of them have only been with Sanctuary Lodges who runs Baines and some other camps, for eight months. He is a trained guide and conservationist (I was surprised, I thought his training would be in hotel management) and a South African. She is from Belgium. Because of the dangers of being in the bush, the staff had to be with us as long as we weren't in our cabins at night. Normally only one would stay with us, but I think Sean and Elka enjoyed our group. We sure think we are fun.

The seven of us sat around the fire under the stars while Elka kept our wine glasses full (I stopped at some point) and told stories and laughed. What a great group of personalities. Axel and Katrine were totally loose now, few vestiges of their Prussian heritage remained. I am really glad we have known them long enough to get to know them this way. We all broke up about 12:30 a.m.; too few hours before our 6 a.m. wake-up call!

I slept outside again on my third and final night at Baines Camp. During the night I heard something off and on I thought could be a lion. Maybe a baboon, or a hippo. Maybe a bird. It's a ways away. No, it's close. Hell, what do I know? I am half awake, half asleep, half intoxicated. Was I dreaming? It turned out to be a lion; it actually walked right through our camp!

The next morning the camp's staff was all abuzz about the lion. When the guides told us that he had passed right through the middle of our camp, very close to the staff quarters and maybe a hundred meters from me, the other guests looked at me like I was crazy for sleeping outside. Linda claims my snoring kept him away.

We were told the lion was likely a male without a pride. He was roaring to reconnect with the rest of his bachelor group who was in the distance on the other side of our camp. Like kids playing "Marco Polo" in a pool, the occasional roar and counter roar would eventually bring the two parties together. This explains why the noise seemed far away initially and then closer as the lone lion moved toward his group on the other side of our camp.

Linda and I were to catch a plane that morning to Kasane, so we packed everything up. I was going on the morning game drive with Axel and Katrine. Linda would stay at the camp to make sure everything was packed up and would be taken to the airstrip to meet me at 10 a.m. in time for our plane.

As we leave the camp in the landie with Ben and Wanko, they show Axel, Katrine and me the lion's tracks through the camp. They looked larger than normal to me, maybe because I was realizing how exposed I had been to him.

Linda thinks my snoring kept him away; I think he probably smelled me and decided he didn't like human meat pickled with red wine. Ben decides we should track him and find him.

Let me digress for a minute. You may have picked up by now, there are no roads in the Okavango Delta, just tracks where other vehicles have punched out over land and through water. For the most part, everything gets covered in water seasonally, which is why there are no permanent roads and one of the reasons the camps aren't permanent. The guides try to use the same tracks wherever possible for environmental reasons.

Back to our morning game drive. Ben has decided we will go in search of the lion. We drive off track following the lion's spoor through grasses, marshes, swamps and water, among trees, over clumps, everywhere and anywhere, stopping at the occasional areas cleared by buffalo and elephants to check for tracks. As we inch through a thicket of trees trying to get from one clearing to another, jostling back and forth, ducking thorns and branches (they really put these landies to the test), Ben suddenly stops, looks down at an isolated mound of dirt, the only clear spot within a half a mile of us, and proclaims the smudge in the soft sand to be our lion's paw print. He is very big, says Ben, and he is headed that way. Oh c'mon! Saddled with skepticism to start with, I leaned back and internally rolled my eyes. At least Ben didn't claim he could smell him!

For thirty more minutes, we jostle around, all seven pairs of eyes searching for the lion, tall grasses and trees making it virtually impossible to see anything let alone a lion unless it was moving. The whole time Ben is making comments similar to those he made the night before; he knows the lion is here, but the tall grasses....

I sense Ben is about to give up when, amazingly, we spot the lion! He is moving through the grass in front of us. Ben had been spot on as to where he would be. Almost impossible to see, except for his movement. The lion moved into the trees just as our landie started making some seriously bad noises; we had picked up a loose wire and it was clanging around under our landie posing some risk to the underside. We wait until the lion gets further away, then Wanko gets out of the landie to remove the wire.

Now wire free, we move on, but we have lost sight of the lion. We drive around a copse of trees to try to spot him on the other side. I am thinking Ben is screwing up royally (there is that lack of confidence, again) when he drives into the copse rather than around it. Then I spot the lion's head barely visible under the trees in the brush. He had laid down, probably for the day. Unless you knew he was there, you couldn't see him unless he raised his head. That's Ben two, Gary zero.

He was a young male with a light-colored mane and Ben admitted he wasn't as big was he thought he would be from the spoor (I won't ding him for that). We stayed with him, watching until another landie from nearby Stanley's

Camp found us from Wanko's radio transmission (I was pretty impressed anyone could actually describe where we were; the other landie couldn't even see us until he was practically upon us).

Okay, so my confidence was restored. These guys really are good. I am a little sheepish for doubting their knowledge of the animals and of the area and the artistic skill they demonstrate in locating them. I tipped them nicely when they handed me off to another landie (with Linda in it driven by Sean) at a pre-arranged spot to be driven to the airstrip. I kissed the lovely Katrine goodbye and warmly shook Axel's hand. We had some great times together. I am sure we will exchange some emails and pictures.

While we sat next to the airstrip in the landie with Sean waiting for our plane, Linda and I had a great opportunity to learn about him and his conservation interests. The same plane with the same pilot that transported us from Maun to Chief's Camp (14-seat, turboprop) landed to take us away. We had a one-half hour flight at 4,500 feet above the ground to Linyanti, Botswana where we landed to pick up a couple (who were going to Tongabezi, as we were). From there we had another forty-five minutes or so due east to Kasane, our last stop in Botswana.

At the Kasane airport, as planned, we were greeted by a guy from an outfit called Bushtracks. This guy had no idea that he was supposed to first drive us to Zimbabwe to see Victoria Falls, and from there, drive us into Zambia and on to Tongabezi Lodge, our final destination for the day. Instead, his instructions said to take us straight to the Zambian border, not the Zimbabwean border. The other couple we had picked up in Linyanti was with us and I didn't want to make an issue with this driver who clearly had no authority and whose written instructions were clear. Oh well, I decided I would deal with the screw-up later with Sandy and Pulse Africa (who we had worked with to arrange the safari portion of our trip). We would figure out a plan B for Zimbabwe.

The border crossing between Botswana and Zambia is over the Zambezi River, probably about twenty miles west (upriver) from Livingstone, Zambia where Victoria Falls is. It was very easy for us, but a nightmare for all the truckers who were lined up along the road for miles on both sides of the border. We understand they wait for three or more days to get across the border. There is a single-truck ferry which crosses the Zambezi. We went across in a private boat owned by Bushtracks; we were to be met by another car and driver on the Zambia side.

The pilot of our boat stopped mid-river to point out the confluence of the Chobe River and the Zambezi River and to show us the four different shorelines of Botswana, Namibia (the Caprivi Strip), Zimbabwe and Zambia. There aren't many places in the world you can stand in one spot and "touch" four countries! We did three countries at the Golden Triangle with Thailand, Laos and Myanmar, and were near three with Brazil, Argentina and Uruguay and possibly places in Europe with three. But, I can't think of other places with four.

Neither side of the river at this border crossing has any dock structures. Our boat and the ferries, simply drive up onto the dirt shoreline. The process of customs and immigration on both sides was easy, except it cost us $135 US each to enter Zambia. We had a forty-five minute van ride from the ferry crossing east toward Livingstone, Zambia and our destination, the Tongabezi Lodge.

It is now 9:45 a.m. I moved from our hut to the lodge's riverside patio a while ago for breakfast. Now, we are about to depart for our helicopter ride over Victoria Falls; should be cool!

— — —

The helicopter ride was just awesome! Helicopters are so cool to start with and it gave us an outstanding perspective on the falls and surrounding area.

At the small heliport, I urged Linda to hop into the front of the helicopter next to the pilot; I would sit in the back with the other two riders. While the rotors were turning, we ducked and hustled up to the open door next to the pilot. Linda hopped into the left front seat, took a look down at her feet and immediately hopped back out, as though she had sat on a bee. She had sat in the seat just long enough to realize that when she looked down to her feet she could see the ground through the glass between them; the helicopter's glass bubble extended all the way below the front seats. Despite my urging, she wanted no part of that! I did. She insisted she was perfectly content in the back.

We got back to Tongabezi Lodge from our helicopter ride about 1:30 p.m. When I got back here I used the Lodge's computer to send a group email home; I hadn't written since the first day at Chief's Camp nearly a week ago:

TONGABEZI LODGE, ZAMBIA
Subject: Bouncing

Hi everybody!

It has been awhile since I have written; it's been a combination of no computer and being busy. Life at a bush camp is hectic! When you aren't eating you are bouncing around in the back of a Land Cruiser.

We start with a wake-up coffee at 6 am; breakfast at 6:30 am; tea in the bush around 10 am; lunch usually around 12:30 pm; tea again at 3:00 pm (have I commented yet on our good fortune that our forefathers broke the bond with Britain?); a "sundowner" in the bush at sunset (now that is a good tradition from wherever it came); dinner at around 8 pm; drinks for as long as you can keep your eyes open; wake-up coffee at 6 am.......you get the idea.

The only exercise you get is trying to keep yourself upright in a bouncing vehicle. Doesn't sound like much exercise until you consider you do it for 7 to 10 hours a day; sometimes up to 5 hours in a stretch. As miserable as it sounds, it goes by fast and is rarely boring. Too many experiences to relate and the pictures will not do any of it justice, but suffice it to say, it is simply magical watching two male lions slurp water from a water hole from 10 yards away with the African landscape and setting sun providing the background.

We enjoyed both Chief's Camp and Baines Camp in the Okavango Delta in Botswana and then arrived by plane, boat and van at the Tongabezi Lodge near the Victoria Falls in Zambia late yesterday (Thursday) afternoon. Tongabezi is considered one of the top 10 honeymoon locations in the world (Linda's reaction: "Really? What the hell are we doing here?" -- where's the romance?). It is truly pretty. Even though we have to be escorted around after dark; they worry about their guests encountering one of the hippo's which exit the river right next to the huts. This place is very civilized although the power is erratic....which means it works occasionally...so I am not sure I will get this off to you before it goes out again or be able to write you again before we leave for the Zambian bush in two days.

We bought two giraffes! Britt, do your kind house-sitting services include Giraffe care? We bought them to keep the hedge maintained. Actually, we bought two hand-carved giraffes for the house which are currently in one piece per giraffe. I expect the pieces will multiply by the hundreds by the time we see them again. But they will go well with our multi-piece elephant from Thailand.

Today we saw Victoria Falls by helicopter; a very convenient---and dry---way to see them; and dramatic. Pretty impressive. At my urging while the rotors were turning, Linda hopped into the left front seat next to the pilot....and then immediately hopped out again when she realized she could see to the ground through the glass at her feet. She wanted no part of that. I did, though!

Afterward we went to a local Zambian primary school to watch the students (5 to 13 years old) put on a demonstration of their traditional dances for some visiting Irish immersion school children. Before the event got started and while we were sitting near the students in the "stands", I pulled out pictures Dennis and Susan had given me from the local traditional village. They took pictures of kids and other villagers when they were here last fall and asked me to bring the pictures back to the village--which I will do tomorrow. Some of the kids from that village go to this little school. Scores of kids huddled around Linda and me to see the pictures, giggling and laughing as they recognized the kids in the pictures. The kids were respectful and careful of the pictures and patiently waited their turn to see the photos. It is, I suspect, a preview of what might happen tomorrow in the village. It was very special to interact with these kids in the manner made possible by Dennis' and Susan's pictures. Thank you Dennis and Susan! Oh, and the dance demonstration was touching and very, very funny. The short videos I took will tell the story.

On Sunday we take off for our three Zambian game camps. Four out of six days without electricity. That is a LOT of bad hair days for Linda. It will be interesting to see how that goes. She is still trying to back out of the hiking camp we have scheduled for our second camp in Zambia. She has quizzed every guide we have come into contact with and even the one rifleman we had on one of our brief walks in Botswana: "How often do you practice? Can you hit anything? But I don't want you to kill the animals." I was waiting for him to shoot her!

But not to worry. I can now identify lion, leopard and hyena tracks....oh, and elephant (looks like a very large mouse pad). I have no idea what to do with that information; a lion will probably bite me in the ass while I am bent over with my face to the ground!

Hopefully we will be able to write again, soon.

Bye for now....

Gary

SATURDAY, MAY 31

Victoria Falls

Brrrr. I am sitting riverside along the Zambezi at the Tongabezi Lodge's "Café Dock" in a swimsuit, T-shirt and flip-flops. It is much too cool to be dressed like this. We leave in an hour (it is now 8 a.m.) to visit Victoria Falls, this time by land. I am dressed to get wet.

After the helicopter ride yesterday, we were taken by the

Tongabezi Lodge van with our guide, Chande, to a craft market. There we saw two hand-carved giraffes that I think would look good in our home; $70 US for both. The proprietor allowed us to take them down the road to the DHL office to get an estimate for shipping them back to the U.S. The giraffes only weigh about ten pounds, but they are fragile. The estimate was $377 US, including insurance. Ugh! I had a $200 US limit in my head, but to his credit, Chande thought it would be more like $300-$400. As we were going through all of this at the DHL desk with the very alluring DHL girl, we noted some flaws in one of the giraffes. We went back to the craft place, picked out a better one and took it back to the DHL place to arrange the shipping. My alluring friend said she thought her estimate was probably a little high, but she didn't want to surprise me. She said she would come by the Tongabezi Lodge around 4 p.m. with the final amount for me to pay. The final amount turned out to be $300 and she assured me she gave the giraffes her own special TLC in the packing. I will be very surprised if they make it to our home intact.

When we got back to the lodge around 1:30 p.m., I walked up to the small school sponsored by the lodge (and funded in part by contributions from its guests, like us). It is the Tujadane School and is for disadvantaged children ages five to thirteen. While there I learned the school children were putting on a dance/song demonstration at 2:30 p.m., so I walked back to the Lodge for lunch and to get Linda.

I returned with Linda in time to watch the demonstration; it was touching and very, very funny. In one of the dances, the boys and girls dance together in a manner adults would consider erotic, but I am quite sure these young boys and girls were just wiggling their hips and having fun. It

was hilarious. It reminded Linda and me of Shaun when he was thirteen years old in Mykonos dancing with an 18-

year old vixen. Too naïve to really know what he was doing, and to our horror, having the time of his life.

Before things got started, I pulled out photographs my business partner, Dennis, and his wife, Susan, had taken of the some of the villagers when they visited eight months or so earlier. The reaction of the children to these photos of themselves and their friends was priceless. Linda had brought with her the things she had to give to kids on these occasions: chalk, stickers, playing cards, etc. She gave it all to Vanessa, the Irish wife of Tongabezi Lodge manager and herself, the director of the Tujadane School.

I came back to the Lodge to meet the alluring DHL girl and to check emails. It was at this time I wrote the email home.

Linda and I re-connected with Angie and Andy from London who we originally bumped into at the Peech Hotel in Johannesburg. We also saw them on the flight to Maun and were surprised to see them again here at the Tongabezi Lodge. We have learned it is a small community of people doing the safari circuit at any one time.

We ate dinner with Angie and Andy and a very obnoxious woman from New Jersey, Teaneck to be exact. She was with her husband. Angie and Andy were really not pleased to be around her. We will avoid her tonight.

After dinner, Linda and I sat around the fire chatting with Angie and Andy. It was a beautiful clear night; the moonlight was shimmering off the smooth-flowing Zambezi River and the occasional grunt from a hippo was the only mar on an otherwise serenely quiet evening. It was getting late, around 11 PM, and I was talking with the lovely Angie about her budding acting career when suddenly it started sprinkling. That was a little shocking, we hadn't seen a cloud in over two weeks and Angie had just commented on how lovely the starlit sky was—and all of a sudden it starts raining? How does that happen? Well, it doesn't. What does happen is that Vervet monkeys will occasionally pee on you. Angie and I got sprinkled rather much. It was off to the showers for us—separate showers (Linda and Angie's idea, not mine).

Off to the falls!

— — —

This morning twelve of us from the Lodge hopped into the van to see Victoria Falls from the water level. It was pretty impressive. I had dressed the way I had because we were warned we might get wet from the spray from the falls. But, they assured us, it "won't be that big of deal." Wrong! It was like standing in a very, very heavy rain in the wind. We ended up getting totally drenched from head to toe.

When we first got to the falls we were able to walk to the edge of the river only ten feet from the top of the falls. At this point, the water eddied around in a pool before dropping over and falling 300 feet! There was no railing and nothing keeping us from wading in the pool of water so close to an unwanted dive into space. I understand on the other side of the river (in Zimbabwe) people actually do that; that is, sit in a pool at the fall's edge, not dive over the edge. Didn't matter what side I was on, I wasn't getting in that water!

From there we walked along a narrow walkway with water pouring over it a mere three feet from the edge of a cliff which faced the falls some fifty meters away. The walkway had no safety rail. Four people die each year at the falls (2 suicide; 2 accidental); it must not be enough to justify investing in a little protection. We walked over a narrow foot bridge spanning a deep gorge facing the roaring falls maybe, again, only 50 meters away. Linda, fortunately, didn't go this far. She could not have handled it. The wind and the rain-mist from the falls were at their worst at this point and two inches of water poured under and over our feet down the sloped walkway of the bridge. On the bridge there were handrails so it wasn't overly treacherous. At the mid-point of the bridge we looked over the rail to see a complete circle rainbow. I didn't know that was possible! Pretty cool.

Completely drenched and exhilarated from our outing, we all shopped around the craft market at the parking lot for the falls before heading back to the Lodge and getting into dry clothes.

After freshening up and relaxing for a short while, we sat with Al and Kathleen from Canada. They have been living with their 9- and 13-year old daughters in Lusaka since last September, the start of Kathleen's two-year assignment there with CARE International. During lunch we agreed we would sit together tonight at dinner with Angie and Andy. We let the staff know we wanted a table set for six.

After eating we went to Simonga Village, about three kilometers away. This is the largest of the Simonga Villages housing 300 of the some 3,000 of the Simonga Tribe. It is a traditional village with mud houses and thatched roofs. There is no electricity and water is hauled from two hand pumps from wells the government provided

about nine years ago. Before that water was hauled by hand three kilometers from the river to the hill on which the village sits. This is the same village Dennis and Susan visited last September (2007) and from which some of the kids attend the Tujadane School we visited yesterday.

Linda and I rode into the village with Rafael from the Tongabezi Lodge, who arranged for us to visit the village. We drove through the village on their dirt streets past many of the villagers' huts to the only non-mud house; it was the village head-woman's house. She is the tribal chief, essentially Simonga royalty. This old wizened woman sat in her chair on her porch as we greeted her. We were appropriately humble, essentially copying whatever we saw Rafael do. We shook her hand by putting our left on our right elbow as though we were lifting and offering our right hand to her. A sign of respect.

We sat and listened to Rafael describe the tribe's customs to us while her highness and her twenty-year old adopted son, Junior, listened. We learned that Rafael is Tonga and that Simonga is an ancient blend of Tonga and a Zambian tribe from the Western province. The tribal customs are very similar so Rafael was at home leading the conversation. We thanked the headwoman for her time, said goodbye and started a walk through the village with Junior. Rafael would meet us at the other end in the van.

As we left Rafael sitting with the headwoman on the porch, she handed him a log to write in. The village gets compensated in some manner for cooperating with these visits. As far as we could tell, not many people visit the village; we were the only ones to do so from Tongabezi.

We were told we could take pictures without concern, but I would always ask before I took photos of villagers. I handed Junior the photographs Dennis and Susan had taken (the same ones we had shown to the children at the Tujadane school) and asked him to give them to the appropriate people as we walked around. The recipients were excited to have actual pictures of themselves or of their family members. We must have walked almost the identical path Dennis and Susan did months before.

There seemed to be a reluctant willingness on the adult's part to have their picture taken, which I usually did with their children. It's as though they are allowing this intrusion because their headwoman instructed them to which she likely does because it is a source of income to the village. We gave $20 US to the village and the same amount to the school. This seemed to be accepted as very generous. I am just not sure how I feel about paying for what may appear to be voyeurism, or should I be asking: Does paying justify the voyeurism? Is it voyeurism? Is satisfying one's intellectual curiosity being voyeuristic? Is that what I am really doing? I'm not sure how to sort through those questions, but I need to feel better about doing it, or not do it anymore.

The Simonga live as humbly as any we have seen. A family will have one hut for adults; sometimes there is more than one wife, one for daughters, a separate one for sons and a toilet enclosure, which I assume is just a hole in the ground). The huts have straw on dirt floors for sleeping and the cooking fires are outside in the middle of the family's circle of huts. Each family is self-sustaining with tasks assigned to women and men based on tradition. The men erect the wood frame for the hut, the women put the mud in for the walls, the women gather the straw for the roof, the men install it, the women get water, and so forth.

Our tour ended at the village's school buildings, which were concrete brick, all built through private donations. Teachers are paid by the state. Education is free through grade seven. We met in the very humble library that was built and supplied by a $10,000 donation from an American. As I said earlier, I left the schoolmaster $20 US and I could see from the log I signed that was considerably more than others had given. The log was more a visitors' register with a column for the amount of donation. I am now realizing I should have asked to look back in the log to see Dennis' name.

After 1½ hours of touring the village, I was able to recover my hand from the little village boy who had insisted on holding it the whole time I was there (very cute) and we went back to Tongabezi Lodge.

SUNDAY, JUNE 1

Linda and Angie enjoying the sunset from the Tongabezi Lodge honeymoon suite

I am under the covered sitting area of our Tongabezi hut looking over the mist covering the Zambezi River, its shore only fifteen feet from me. It is not quite 8 a.m.

The hippos were more active close to our hut last night than they have been on previous nights. Yesterday morning, based on some ill-conceived notion, Linda and I walked out of our hut and in our robes with coffee and camera in hand looking for hippos. Fortunately we saw none, but we saw tracks within yards of our hut where they had re-entered the water after using the cover of night to sneak inland to feed on grasses on the grounds of the Lodge and beyond. Woken by grunts last night I felt and heard one rumble by and then splash into the water; he might have been spooked by something. Despite all the near encounters with hippos, both here and at Baines Camp, I have yet to see one out of the water in any proximity. That is likely a good thing; hippos are responsible for more human deaths in Africa than any other animal.

Around noon today, we will leave Tongabezi via the Livingstone airport to go to Zambia's capital city, Lusaka, and then on to Chongwe River Camp, getting there around 4 p.m.

Yesterday, after returning from Simonga Village, I showered, sent an email to Pulse Africa about the Zimbabwean mix-up, checked emails and then wrote in my journal while sitting along the Zambezi River.

At 5:30 p.m., as scheduled, Linda and I went to Tongabezi's signature honeymoon suite where Angie and Andy were staying. We had ordered drinks and wine to be sent to the suite so we could enjoy the sunset from there with them. My God, what a great hut, er suite! It was all open in the front with a private courtyard maybe 25 feet above water level. It was an amazing setting. We had a nice time chatting with them as we watched the sun go down over the Zambezi River.

After our sunset cocktails, we went to the fire pit next to the dining area. Because of the way the seats were arranged around the fire, we were separated from Angie and Andy by two other couples already seated there. I sat and had an engaging conversation about China with an architect from Kansas. When everyone else moved to the candle-lit tables for dinner, I remained engrossed in my conversation. Minutes later when I went to our table I could see that five people were seated already; good, I am thinking, Al and Kathleen made it as planned. Only it wasn't Al and Kathleen seated at our table, it was the Jewish couple from Teaneck, New Jersey, one of whom of course was Mary, Andy's least favorite person.

Before that while having sunset drinks at the honeymoon suite I kidded with Andy about having invited Mary and her husband to eat with us at dinner. He saw no humor in that whatsoever; he really despises that woman. I came clean and told him I hadn't invited them, instead I had invited Al and Kathleen, who, like the rest of us, he really enjoys. And now I am coming up to the table, and horror of horrors, Mary is sitting right next to Andy! I didn't know if I should laugh or cry. When I sat down, I looked at him, widened by eyes and shrugged my shoulders in question. I had no idea why they were seated with us, but just assumed Mary, consistent with her personality, simply felt entitled to sit wherever she wanted. After my shoulder shrug, Andy looked at me and said aloud, "I would rather be eating my toe nail clippings." A classic barb I will forever remember. As I assume Andy intended, Mary heard what he had said, but didn't seem to understand the comment was made about her.

When Al and Kathleen showed up, we pushed another table next to us and I sat with them not really seeing any way to get Andy and Angie to my table. It was pure anguish for him.

After dinner we all moved back to the fire pit, where I actually had a nice conversation with Mary's husband. Eventually, fearing another nighttime monkey shower, I headed for bed.

Time for breakfast.

— — —

After breakfast this morning, we went with Al, Kathleen and an Australian guest we had met, to see the treehouse hut where Al and Kathleen were staying. The riverside hut the Linda and I are staying in is quaint, cute and perfect for us, but it isn't one of the handful of "special" huts the Tongabezi has. The treehouse hut, like the honeymoon suite, is pretty glamorous and exotic, but not something I would value. I took pictures to email Al and Kathleen since they had no camera.

Linda was asking the Australian at breakfast if he was using Bushtracks to get to the airport today (that being the company we are using). Apparently unaware of the company, he said, "No, actually the road to the airport is pretty good!" Pretty funny.

TUESDAY, JUNE 3

Greater Kudu seen near Chongwe River Camp in Zambia

I am sitting in front of our tent at the Chongwe River Camp. It is 1 p.m. We just finished lunch and have a couple of hours before our afternoon activity, which will be a sunset cruise on the river. We arrived here Sunday, two days ago, and have spent two nights here; I have some catching up to do.

Our departure from Tongabezi and the Livingstone airport two days ago was all smooth. On our flight into Lusaka there was a fun, boisterous group of five young people aboard our twelve-seat turboprop aircraft. While I was talking to one of the girls of the group, one of the other members of the group asked if I knew I was talking to the current Miss Zambia. She was traveling with her camera crew and, as you would expect, was tall and gorgeous. I can't believe I didn't get a picture with her.

Linda, unable to wait an hour for food we have already paid for, had to go into the airport in Lusaka to buy two sandwiches to go. $30 US later for two cracker-size, dried out, terrible sandwiches, we were boarding a 1950's twin engine piston plane for our 35-minute flight to Royal Air Strip. As we approached, the pilot circled the landing strip to be sure it was clear before landing; this strip did not

have guides in landies hanging around to shoo away critters. We landed, deplaned and after a fifteen-minute landie ride we were at the Chongwe River Camp. This camp is near the mouth of the Chongwe River, on its west bank, perhaps a mile from where it pours into the Zambezi River. We are west-northwest of, probably around 250 miles downriver from, Victoria Falls. I am presently looking across the Zambezi River into the Lower Zambezi National Park.

We were met when we arrived to the camp by the sexy Storm, who manages the camp with her hubby, Rob, or "Ox", as he is called. A good-looking, broad-shouldered guy. Both in their early thirties and South Africans. They are very nice, and a lot of fun.

The Chongwe River Camp is just awesome. There are only nine tents. They are widely-spaced and are strung along the three-foot bank of the Chongwe River. Our tent, number 4, is only twenty feet from the water and about 100 feet from the hippos lounging in the middle of this small, slow, moving river.

This camp is more rustic than our previous camps. Here the open-sided tents sit on concrete bases (apparently not restricted in that regard as they were in the Okavango) and have thatched shelters built over the top of them. The tents have mosquito mesh on the sides with roll down canvas on the inside for privacy. From the back sides of the tents, you enter the open-air bomas where the bathrooms are. The boma enclosures are only about five feet high and have no roofs over them. So when I shower, or stand at the sink or at the toilet, I can see out to anyone who happens to be looking in! Everything done in the bathroom is done in the open air. The camp's generator runs only the one light in each of the tents and one in each of the bomas. Water is heated by tiny gas units. Each night they bring an oil lantern to your tent; you light and swing this lantern to catch the attention of the night guard if you need help or need to leave your tent for any reason. There are two camp chairs and a tiny table sitting in the sand in front of the tent a

mere twenty feet from the Chongwe River bank; the water is only three feet lower.

We have had wildlife near us at all of our camps (even Tongabezi); this one is by far the busiest, and noisiest. That is due mostly to the hippos which I can see right now sunning themselves 75 meters away on the opposite shore of the Chongwe. Baboons are squealing at this very moment (and most other moments). I look to my left and see two elephants 400 meters away on my side of the Chongwe. The night before we arrived, an elephant destroyed tent number 9; the tent was in the way of the tree branches it was wanting to get to. And yesterday an elephant strolled through camp during the day—Linda was within feet of him as she stood in the dining boma not knowing what to do. More on that later.

Generally speaking, elephants, baboons and the many birds I can hear at the moment go silent at night. It is the hyenas and hippos that make most of the noise at night. The hippos make plenty of noise during the day, too. The wheeze and snort, snort, snort of a hippos is loud, distinct and memorable; I have even gotten reasonably good at imitating their sound.....

Hold on.....something is going on with the baboons. They are going nuts. I had better pay attention for a moment. They could be reacting to a threat, a lion, leopard...maybe a black mambo snake. Ok, back now. All clear.

I am going to miss the "hippo music" when I return home. The hippos lounge around in or near the water all day, then after night falls, they leave the water and go inland up to six miles to graze all night, returning just before daylight. They return to the water following their outbound tracks; to the point that their combined track is not much wider than one of the pads on their feet. They must walk in a manner in which each hippo puts all four feet in line. And somehow, that track is followed by all the hippos in a group. The track they leave is well under two feet wide, and many inches deep. I am looking at two tracks now, one is fifteen meters to my right, another the same distance to my left (there are many others).

Each night I have heard the hippos' wheeze, snort, snort, snort near my tent. Last night I raised my head to look out the side of our open tent to see the shadowy hulk of a hippo lumbering by not twenty feet away. The herd followed, single file, the dominant male in the lead. The vibration from their padding feet shook our bed. A little ominous, but very cool.

When Linda and I first arrived at Chongwe River Camp two days ago, on Sunday, about 4 p.m. we took a cruise on the river. The boat we used was an open twenty foot aluminum boat with a small outboard motor...

...I just heard a hippo splash in the water across the Chongwe and I can see a huge crocodile (longer than the hippo) laying on the shore sunning himself. Sorry for these interruptions, sitting here writing is like sitting in a zoo---on the wrong side of the enclosure!

In any event, it was a very pleasant cruise in a small boat on the calm waters of the river with two ladies who were visiting from Kafunta Camp in South Luangwa Park. We returned from our boating excursion, showered and went to the eating area of the Chongwe Camp where we met Nadia and Theo, who now live in Amsterdam (Theo is Dutch). Nadia is a randy Siberian who is a bit past her prime (but not too far). We have had all of our game drives since being here at Chongwe with them as well as a canoe adventure. They are nice enough and fun to be around. We have spent the two nights at dinner and around the fire pit with them, getting to know them but also getting to know Storm and Rob.

Storm and Rob met in college, got married and then returned to their home country in N.E. South Africa to start macadamia nut farming. Two years ago the South African government bought their farm pursuant to some program, which gave Storm and Rob no choice but to sell at what the government determined was market price. Long story short, they got into managing game camps; first in Tanzania for 1½ years and now here for two months so far. They seem perfectly suited for it.

Yesterday morning (Monday), our first at Chongwe, we got up at 5:45 a.m. to be able to start our game drive at 6:45 a.m. Sunrise is around 6 a.m.

The terrain and scenery is much different here in Zambia than at the Okavango Delta; greener and hillier with much different foliage. This side of the Chongwe River is a Game Management Area (GMA), the other is the Lower Zambezi National Park, so each morning, we cross the Chongwe River into the Park. The GMA acts as a buffer to keep poachers from sitting on the river banks to shoot wildlife in the Park. The land can be privately owned in the GMA and villages exist inside it, but not in the Park. The highlight of our first morning game drive was seeing a huge, fifteen-lion pride.

After returning from the game drive and having lunch, I tried to nap and write in my journal (not at the same time), but I got interrupted by an elephant in the camp. The staff named this elephant "Oliver" because of a twist in its tail. He happens to be a relatively well behaved boy which is a good thing because he started to stroll right into the camp's eating boma where Linda and Nadia were sitting talking. There was no other staff around. Fortunately, the elephant decided to skip going into the eating area and went along its side, within mere yards of the two women. By the time I got there (reacting from 100 yards away to the restrained yelling of the two women), Oliver was casually destroying some shrub, eating it right next to the boma. I took some photos. Oliver eventually moved on.

Later that day, Nadia, Theo, Linda and I went canoeing. Our regular guide, Richman (yes, I am spelling that correctly) took the girls in one canoe and Theo and I oared the other. It was an easy, gorgeous, serene downriver float for 1½ hours. Another canoe with a guide, a mother and her twelve year old daughter (Fiona and Tatyana) followed us. We canoed into the Park where we got out of the canoes just before sunset and from there hopped into a landie for the night drive.

Except for the night drive when we saw the hyenas in the Okavango that night's drive was the most active I have had. We saw jackals, mongooses, genets (cat-like animal related to the mongoose), bush babies (little night monkeys) and a porcupine to name those I can think of at the moment. And we had a great location and wonderful time during our stop for our "sundowner". We got back to the Chongwe River Camp around 8 p.m.

We all went straight to the camp's fire pit and were served drinks.....

.....here we go again; a huge bull elephant just stepped to the shore on my side of the Chongwe River to drink, maybe 150 meters away. What a pretty scene for an early afternoon setting! Picture time.

I just spent twenty minutes watching that elephant cross the river, swimming for some portion of the crossing. When he got to the other side (the side of the Lower Zambezi National Park) he began tearing the opposite bank apart, throwing mud everywhere. I have no idea why he would do that.

Anyway, last night ended early, around 10:30 p.m. without fanfare or any great stories. It had been a long and very fun day.

The following morning, this morning, just Theo and I went on the morning drive, waking at 5:30 a.m. and leaving the camp at 6 a.m. The early departure made no improvement in the results; it was a nice drive but that was about it. We returned to camp, ate lunch and then I came to sit along the river bank at our hut to write in my journal. I have had more excitement sitting here writing in my journal than the game drive this morning!

Time to get ready for 3:30 p.m. tea and the 4 p.m. river cruise.

THURSDAY, JUNE 5

Zebras seen during a walking safari from Chikoko Camp

It is early afternoon and I am sitting on the "porch" of our tent in Tafika Camp in Zambia. Once again it has been two day's since I have written so I have a lot to catch up on.

Our last night, two nights ago (Tuesday night) at Chongwe River Camp was fun. We met Barney and Jenny (honeymooners from London) during our 4 p.m. river cruise that evening. It was just the four of us and George, the river guide. Before engaging in our all-important sundowner while floating downriver, we spotted the largest herd of elephants we have seen. There were maybe 75 of them on the river's shoreline.

After dinner, I had a lengthy, and personal, conversation with Storm and Ox about their careers and life plans. Personal, not because I asked, but because they seemed eager to talk about it. They are young, intelligent and flexible, and they appear to both be in agreement about how they move forward with new challenges. They are a great couple.

The next morning (Wednesday) after a very warm goodbye from Storm and Ox, Linda and I were taken to the Royal Air Strip for our 9 a.m. charter flight to Mfuwe. It was a twin-engine Islander, a fixed gear, variable-pitch propped aircraft with combustion engines; the same kind of plane we flew in to the Royal Air Strip from Lusaka three days earlier. I rode right seat up front in the plane with Danny, the British pilot. We first flew 25 minutes northeast to the other end of Lower Zambezi Park to drop another

passenger off. As we neared touchdown at that runway some Impala had not cleared the runway, so we had to go-around. On our next approach the runway remained clear and we were able to land fine. Then on the ground, we once again had to wait for the Impala to move out of the way before we could taxi to the end of the runway to take off again. I kept my eyes (as I am sure Danny was) alert for the Impala as we started our take-off roll; hitting one on the runway would likely ruin both our days!

We had about an hour flight to Mfuwe. As we climbed to 9,500 feet, the pilot noting my interest and awareness of the instrument panel, asked if I had flown. I told him about my pilot's license, quickly followed by qualifying statements about my limited flying experience. He nodded and offered to let me take the controls. I flew the plane all the way to Mfuwe. As we neared our destination, Danny pointed to the airstrip out our right window and told me to get lined up on the runway and to lower my altitude. With no assistance from Danny, except for telling me the altitude and when I should add flaps, I lined the plane up on final approach with a perfect attitude for landing (yes, I impressed myself!). As we passed through 500 feet, I begin to think he is going to have me land the plane (was I sufficiently impressed for that?!) Wisely, he took the plane over shortly after. It was fun. Linda, the only passenger, wasn't even aware I was flying the plane.

On the ground, Ernst from Tafika Camp met us and we started our 1½ hour drive to the Chikoko Bush Camp (which is owned and run by Tafika Camp), our next stop on our Zambian adventure. We would be at Chikoko for only one night.

The plans had changed. We were supposed to drive to Tafika Camp and then have a three-hour hike into the Chikoko Bush Camp. Instead, they drove us to the shores of the Luangwa River, where we canoed across and then walked about a mile into the camp. I am not sure why they changed the plans, but so much for Chikoko being an isolated camp; I mean a mile hike versus a three-hour hike? Actually, it is still pretty isolated with no roads into or near the camp on its side of the Luangwa River. Unlike all the other game camps at which we had stayed, or will stay, Chikoko Bush Camp is a hiking camp. The game drives will be game hikes.

Both the Chikoko Bush Camp and the Tafika Camp are inside the South Luangwa National Park, which is the eastern portion of Zambia near the border with Malawi. Both camps are on the western shore of the Luangwa River.

Before our first short hike to get into the Chikoko Bush Camp, we had to canoe across the Luangwa River. The crossing of this swift moving river was a little wild. Loitering in the middle of the river was a herd of six or seven hippos which we had to get past. We have learned that hippopotamuses are responsible for more human deaths in Africa than any other animal; way more than crocodiles, lions and other cat predators and even more than the greatly feared elephant. Hippos can't see, smell or hear worth a damn and with the brain the size of a walnut they pretty much interpret everything as a potential threat. So, hippos tend to charge anything they sense near them. The man rowing our canoe kept a wary eye on the herd and gave them a wide berth as he first rowed Linda and me across the river. Then he rowed back across the river to get our guide and our bags.

At about the half-way point of their return trip to our side, with our guide and luggage aboard, one of the hippos turned to face the canoe, snorted and lunged toward it. When the hippo disappeared below the surface it was safe to assume it was making an underwater charge. This, at least, is how the rower and guide interpreted it. Seeing the rower's arms start churning like a powered windmill would have been funny, had it not been for the look of abject fear on his face and the panic stricken look on our guide's face. They knew all too well the danger they were in and I started to realize it as well. Selfishly, I began to wonder what Linda and I were going to do alone in the African bush if these men didn't make it to shore. I can't convey this story in a way to do justice to the true threat these men faced. It was clear from their behavior and mannerisms once they safely got to shore that they believed they had dodged a serious bullet.

The mile-long walk from river's edge to Chikoko Bush Camp allowed an opportunity for everyone's nerves to settle. Except for Linda's; her nervous-meter went tilt again when she saw the night's accommodations. Our hut was a glorified two-story bamboo stick house. It was open on all sides, had a dirt floor, no power and no running water. The camp was decorated with a chair or two and some pillows, but was basically, well, pretty basic.

We had arrived to the camp around 1:30 p.m., so after a little lunch, we relaxed for a while then I took off on our first walking safari with Isaac, a rifleman and Angela, a British woman traveling solo. Linda wisely decided not to go; she would not have much enjoyed the difficult walking. We were scheduled to get back well before dark. The walking was over surprisingly torturous ground, but not hard or strenuous. The weather was perfectly pleasant. We spotted some zebra, puku (a medium-size antelope), waterbucks (large antelope) and a whole bunch of yellow-billed storks, hundreds and hundreds of them. We also had a little excitement.

It is required that a park ranger carrying a rifle accompany any walking safaris in Zambia. Our rifle-toting ranger became anxious on this first hike when an aggressive cow elephant charged toward us.

She was the matriarch determined to protect her breeding herd and its calves. The ranger didn't have to tell me, Angela and Isaac twice to turn and go the other way. The ranger positioned himself between us and the herd, his rifle off his shoulder and leveled toward Big Momma. After the elephant could see we weren't going to threaten her herd, she backed away. But, we ended up having to walk clear around the lake we were near to avoid her and to get back to camp. The extra walking meant we got back to camp much later than expected and after dark. Linda was back at camp with only two male, non-English speaking cooks so there was no one to explain to her why we might be late or that the rifle shots she was hearing were not from my group, but from an area miles away where hunting is allowed. Her nervous-meter was bouncing on the pegs by the time I strolled into camp. She was not interested in my exuberance or my stories from my little hike. Nope, not at all.

That night, with just Isaac, Angela, Linda and me, and a couple of local men off somewhere cooking for us, it was a real quiet night. We ate in the dark, on the dirt, near the fire next to the river bank of a little creek passing by our camp. Angela is a nice lady. Her brother used to work for John and Carol Coppinger who own Chikoko and Tafika Camps. He is currently at Tafika while she spends a couple of nights at Chikoko. She has a big job; she runs one of the subway lines of the London Underground.

We went to bed early; the night was uneventful despite essentially sleeping exposed to all the elements. Needless to say, given the events of the afternoon, Linda's sleep that night was a little unsettled. She says she didn't' sleep at all and is convinced a herd of hippos walked through our camp during the night followed shortly by a pride of lions. I don't mean to be unsympathetic, but my dreams were more interesting. They involved a woman named Jane who insisted on calling me Tarzan---and this irritating little chimp....

We got up early the next morning (this morning) for a 4½-hour morning game walk. Again, Linda wasn't interested. We had a close encounter with a giraffe, three hippos at three different times and a herd of four elephants, which once again, we had to walk around extending the duration of our walk.

After I returned to Chikoko Camp from our walking safari, Linda and I gathered our things, hiked back to the Luangwa River, canoed across it (uneventfully this time) and took a landie to Tafika Camp where I am now.

We got here about noon in time for lunch and I have been sitting at the front of our tent since then catching up in my journal, which I now am. Our tent here at Tafika Camp is the "honeymoon suite". From what I can tell, the only difference from other tents is that it is near the edge of the camp away all the others.

I need a quick nap before our afternoon/evening game drive begins.

FRIDAY, JUNE 6

A micro flight does a "fly-by" of Tafika Camp

It is noon now on our second and final day at Tafika Camp; our final day in the bush. I worried after planning this trip a month ago that we had too many days in the bush. But now I know it wasn't. While not too many nights, I might have mixed them up a wee bit differently; adding more diverse locations like the Kalahari Desert.

It seems any days in the bush without the capacity of a hairdryer is too many for Linda. I may have to do this safari thing on my own next time! These past camps in Zambia were among my favorite, but Linda's least because they can't accommodate hair dryers.

When I first arrived here at Tafika yesterday around noon, I was dog tired. We ate lunch and, sitting on the porch of our "honeymoon suite", I forced myself to get caught up in my journal (which I will have to go re-read to see if it is legible and makes sense!), and then I crashed for an hour before the 4 p.m. game drive started. Even then, I had trouble shaking my tiredness. It was weird.

Yesterday, Cameron was our evening guide at Tafika; we went with Jerry and Erin from San Francisco. They are probably late sixties, early seventies, and have brought with them two of their children and ten of their grandchildren, who are generally in their twenties. They are a nice couple. For their send-off (it was the family's last night), Tafika Camp arranged a group sundowner. So, three landies, full of their family and Linda and me, all met in the middle of a plain to have our group sundowner. Not my favorite, I prefer the quiet, serene, get-in-touch-with-your-surrounding sundowner, but it was nice for the family.

After spending much of the night drive last night searching for the elusive leopard that was supposed to be about, we returned to Tafika Camp to find out a leopard had just been inside the camp! We had some good chuckles over dinner about spending hours looking for a leopard just to return to see one laying by the entrance to the camp thumping his tail, impatiently wondering where we had all been! Pretty funny, but also a reminder that there is nothing to keep these predators and others out of our camps. Our isolated "honeymoon suite" is right next to the camp's edge and a good fifty meters from anyone else's tent! I am feeling more like leopard-bait than a honeymooner!

That night around the campfire at Tafika, we were chatting with several of the twenty-something granddaughters of Jerry and Erin and some of the staff and guides. We had a hilarious conversation about the dumbest questions asked of a guide. For whatever reason, I thought it necessary to relate my own experience in this category. On one of my first game drives in the Okavango, when I was alone (fortunately) in the landie with the guide, we spotted and were watching a pride of lions. I noted something I thought unusual and asked the guide why that female lion had such large balls. The very second the words passed my lips, I wanted a do-over. I momentarily forgot my own golden rule: engage your brain, then your mouth. Male lions don't start growing their mane until they are four or five years old. It is true that I didn't know that at the time, but a thoughtful person would have asked the more prudent question: Why doesn't that male lion have a mane? But nooooo, not me. Everyone loved my story, but believe it or not, it didn't come close to winning the dumbest question award.

A definite highlight of safaris is that the enthralling game drives each day are capped by enchanting evenings at the game camps. Dinner is generally a game meat—kudu, crocodile, Cape Buffalo, impala—and there is always plenty of wine. After dinner around the traditional campfire, we are entertained by a harmony of African night sounds, crickets, frogs, hippos and a bunch of things I don't recognize (and may not want to know about). The night sky is filled with Fruit Bats and Southern hemisphere constellations. And, of course, there are the safari stories, told by travelers and guides alike, all of which get better and better with each sip of wine.

One of the attributes of Tafika Camp is that John Coppinger, the camp owner (who looks just like my friend Alan Roberts), pilots a micro light aircraft and offers rides to camp guests. It was the option of the micro light flight that made me choose this camp, but before I did, I was careful to be sure the small aircraft could accommodate my not-so-small, 6'4", 225-pound frame. I was at the upper limit.

My flight was at 6:15 this morning. We walked out to a grassy clearing from where the small aircraft would take off. For those of you who don't know, a micro light aircraft is essentially a lounge chair with wheels. Behind where you sit, a lawnmower engine powers the push-propeller. John hooked me up with a visored helmet and a headset so he and I could talk during the flight. I scrunched into the rear position with John nestled between my legs in the pilot's seat; it was rather cozy. The takeoff run was short and we were quickly in the air. We flew low--as low as 15 feet over crocodiles in the Luangwa

River--and never much higher than 100 feet. After a couple of weeks of ground-level game drives, seeing the animals, birds and terrain from the air was so different and exhilarating. We zoomed around for twenty minutes or so enjoying simply awesome sightseeing. Then, we buzzed the camp, waving at the guests, and landed back at the grass field. It was the most fun I have had with a man between my legs.

After my micro flight, Linda and I took off with Alex for the morning game drive from Tafika Camp. Alex is Zambian from the nearby village of Mkasanga, which Tafika Camp does so much to support. This is his second year as a guide having worked his way up from a spotter and passing the final Zambian guide test. He has a real nose for game and has a great personality. It wasn't long before he found a pride of seventeen lions, eleven of which were cubs. The pride appeared to be resting after eating something. Our landie was between them and a lily-covered pond with four to six hippos in it. On the other side of the pond was a large group (a congress) of baboons frolicking around while keeping a watchful eye on the pride of lions. This whole setting was incredible; and we were in the midst.

We returned to Tafika Camp and before lunch I managed to use the camp's computer to send a group email home:

TAFIKA CAMP, ZAMBIA
Subject: The African Bush

Hello from the bush,

I have survived a mock charge from a protective mother elephant while on foot and a flight over a crocodile-infested lagoon in a lounge chair with a lawnmower engine. But Linda's plight has, in her estimation, been insufferably worse: she has survived 5 days, 12 hours and 21 minutes without a hair dryer. As harrowing as my experiences were, I will be fine. Linda, on the other hand, may require psychological treatment when we get home. I have never seen anyone so addicted to electricity. She would know true peace and tranquility only if she could plug herself directly into Grand Coulee Dam.

Seriously everything is great with us. Down to our last night in the bush, one night in Johannesburg, a night in an airplane, and then home.

I have no idea what day of the week it is. The computer says it is 6 June and it is now about 3 am for you all on that day. It is noon of our last day at Tafika Camp.

Two nights ago we were in a glorified two story tent without access by a vehicle. It had open sides, a dirt floor, no power and no running water. Linda is convinced a herd of hippos walked through our tent that night shortly followed by a pride of lions. My dreams were more interesting....they involved a woman named Jane who insisted on calling me Tarzan.

This morning I did a micro flight which for those of you who don't know involves sitting in a lawn chair with wheels and a lawnmower engine at your back attached to a propeller. It is, of course, a much more stable machine than that and the flight at very low altitudes over the terrain and the animals was great fun.

I need to free up this computer so I will sign off. Again, all is well with us and we will try to write again before we leave Africa.

Gary

After I got that email off, we lunched with John Coppinger, his wife, Carol and Judith, a young, cute travel agent from Netherlands. It was nice having so much personal time getting to know John and Carol. They are true legends in the business and history of Zambian game camps. We chatted for a couple of hours. Since then, I have been catching up in my journal.

It is now 3 p.m., time to go to the Mkasanga Village.

SATURDAY, JUNE 7

A giraffe near Tafika Camp in Zambia

It is the end of the line. I am currently aboard a twin-engine turbo prop on our way to Lusaka from Mfuwe. After a 5:30 a.m. wake-up call, we left Tafika Camp at 6:45 a.m. to be driven by Cameron to the Mfuwe airport; it took an hour and forty-five minutes.

— — —

Now, I am sitting in Lusaka's airport. It is 11:15 a.m. Our flight to Johannesburg leaves around 2 p.m.

Yesterday, Linda and I enjoyed an hour's worth of celebrity at the Mkasanga Village. Three hundred kids sat on the ground awaiting our arrival and every eye followed us as we were ushered in to sit in front of them. The school director introduced us in their local language and then several dances and songs were performed for us; a couple of which were hilarious and had everyone laughing. Afterwards, I stood and said thank you and made a few comments which the school director translated for the crowd.

We had expressed an interest at Tafika Camp in seeing a local village (much as we had done in Livingstone). John Coppinger, Tafika Camp's owner, contacted the Mkasanga school director, Francis, who arranged our visit. Linda and I had no idea what to expect, but wanted nothing more than to have someone walk through the village with us. So, we were shocked to see villagers gathered to perform for us.

After the group gathering, we were led through the village for a tour and for a demonstration of how the villagers make flour from sorghum. We were continuously surrounded by scores of villagers, mostly children. We took pictures of them, and some were taken of us—digital cameras were a novelty to them. As we backed away to take our leave, a few of the kids started saying, "Linda, Linda, Linda" and the chant was taken up by all of the kids and other villagers. We could hear them still chanting as our landie was leaving the village.

Later, John said it was not the first time camp guests had gone into the village, but he said it was a rarity. He was surprised at the way Francis had organized it and was amused to hear of our reception. As we did for the village near Livingstone, we left money as a donation for the village's school.

After we left the village, our landie was met by another to take Linda back to Tafika Camp to shower while I went on my last game drive with Cameron and Oman, the spotter. As the three of us drove off, a group of baboons sat on their haunches watching us drive by. My hand automatically went up to wave to them. I guess I still had the "parade-wave" mentality from the village. Realizing what I was doing, I jerked my hand back down, relieved no one had seen me.

As we drove on, I was totally enjoying the beautiful evening. It was 4:45 p.m. or so, the sun would set around 6 p.m. It was a windless evening and a perfect temperature. I was very aware that this was my last time in a landie on this trip and was feeling a little melancholy.

Cameron stopped the landie along the shore of the Luangwa River and we watched what appeared to be an imminent fight between two hippos. They were in the water, maybe thirty meters offshore. Cameron told me a female was staring down a dominant male to protect her young male offspring. I was totally enthralled; hippos, for some reason, really interest me. Most of the activity was occurring with only their snouts and eyes visible above the water, but there was a number of feints and counter-moves between the two large animals while the young male had enough sense to stay behind mommy. It is common for dominant males to try to eliminate future competition by maiming or killing other males while they are young.

After a while, we heard baboons giving an alarm bark (yes, I have come to learn to distinguish that sound from other baboon barks). An alarm bark could only mean one thing, Cameron said, a leopard. We broke away in the waning light, leaving the hippos to their stand-off, to investigate what alarmed the baboons.

We bumped around trying to see through the high grass and across a gulley separating us from the baboons. The baboons were continuing their barking. We gave up when we lost the day's light. We decided to drive around a little more before returning to camp. With the spotlight scanning the area's around us as we bounced along in the landie, Cameron and I talked softly about the kind of wildlife we have in Washington Stare. Oman was working the light.

Suddenly, he spotted the leopard. It was tough terrain, but we motored right up to her as she sauntered through the grass, stopping occasionally to look, listen and sniff; she was hunting. She was an amazingly beautiful animal. We watched her for fifteen minutes before leaving her to her hunting; we had to be out of the Reserve by 8 p.m.

On the way back to camp in the dark, we spotted two civets, a small, badger-like nocturnal mammal (which I had yet to see), a cobra (another first) and a clear view of a bush baby (very unusual). It was a very successful, and great, last drive!

We had bragging rights in camp that night. Linda and I ate with Angela (from Chikoko Camp), Judith (the travel agent) and some of the Tafika Camp staff. We had fun conversations and went to be around 10 p.m.

SUNDAY, JUNE 8

Our plane from Livingstone to Lusaka

I was last writing yesterday while sitting at the Lusaka airport. We left there pretty much on time at 2 p.m. and arrived in Johannesburg at 4 p.m. We grabbed our bags and a taxi and headed to the Peech Hotel. We got here by 5 p.m. on Saturday night. After I arrived, I sent off a group email home to let everyone know we had survived the bush:

> ***JOHANNESBURG, SOUTH AFRICA***
> ***Subject: Safely (?) in Johannesburg***
>
> *Hello all!*
>
> *We have arrived in Johannesburg. I was going to say having survived the African bush, but Johannesburg is probably ten times as dangerous!*
>
> *We only have tonight (Saturday) and tomorrow in*

Johannesburg before catching an evening plane to start our journey home through London. We should arrive in Seattle around 5 pm on Monday.

What an incredible trip it has been. Although we had no checklist of animals to see, the list of animals we didn't see is much shorter. In fact I can name only the Rhinoceros and Honey Badger as the critters we didn't see. It was not, of course, all about the animals. The guides were without exception amazingly knowledgeable, concerned about conservation, sensitive to the animals, aware of safety and fun to be with. We spent a LOT of hours with them and enjoyed every one of them. The other travelers we met were great fun as well. A diverse lot, but mostly Americans and Brits...oh, and one really hot German!

And, the fun of it all was in the hunt. Tracking an animal by examining spoor, listening to the alarms baboons and birds give each other in the presence of a predator and the reaction of Impala, Kudu and other prey when danger is near is all extraordinarily interesting to me and gives such interesting insight into the behavior of various animals. It was enlightening to learn the social and mating habits of various animals. How they prevent inter-breeding, how they assure only the fittest procreate, etc.

We also learned how easy and safe it is to travel in parts of Africa. Each time we travel somewhere we seem to add places to our list of future destinations, and this trip was no exception--places we would never have previously considered (mostly because we'd hardly heard of them!).

I am writing this from the Peech Hotel in Johannesburg, a very quaint boutique hotel...with electricity. We arrived about 5 pm....Linda has been drying her hair for going on 2 hours....just because she can. We will be going into downtown Johannesburg for dinner so I had better get ready to head out.

We will talk to you again from Seattle.

Gary

I am now sitting in the Peech Hotel's breakfast room at 8 a.m. on Sunday morning.

Yesterday, our flights were uneventful. We were the only two people aboard the flight from Mfuwe to Lusaka. I didn't fly the plane and I didn't have Miss World sitting on my lap. Flying from Lusaka to Johannesburg, we flew first over Lake Kariba behind the Kariba Dam on the Zambezi River, maybe a hundred miles downriver from Victoria Falls. And then we flew over Zimbabwe where from the air the terrain looks much more interesting than anything we saw in Botswana and Zambia. I would like to travel Zimbabwe some day after things get a little more settled politically.

When we got to the Peech Hotel last night, we spent some time re-packing since we had recovered our big luggage from the Peech Hotel who held them for us while we were in the bush. We then took long, hot showers (it is clear weather, but a little chilly in Johannesburg). It was while Linda was showering that I used the hotel's computer to write a last email home.

We sat in the Peech's bar for a drink before hailing a taxi to go to Sandton City in Johannesburg. I know so little about Johannesburg, I don't know if Sandton City is an area of the city or the name of a development. It has office buildings, a shopping mall, the Michelangelo Hotel (fancy place) and an area with just restaurants. The office buildings are called the Nelson Mandela Towers and there is a huge statue of him in the mall. It was only ten minutes away (50 Rand or $7 US).

We were headed into the restaurant mall, which is just what you would expect: huge restaurants with picture menus, catering to large groups, families and tourists. But, we knew nowhere else and didn't want to eat at the Peech Hotel. We ate at a beef place, at which neither of us could finish our meals, and then went to the lobby bar of the Michelangelo Hotel. I wasn't much fun. For some reason I was way sleepy the whole night and could only think about bed, which we got to around 11 p.m.

I have seen some very attractive local women and good-looking local men on this trip, but mostly in Zambia, as I think about it. The mix of South Africans we saw last night was entertaining to be sure, but not head-turning. They were either garishly outfitted or blue-collar looking. Perhaps it was just the “mall crowd”, but we saw some doozies last night!

I need to consider a plan for the day. We won’t leave for the airport until 6 p.m. and aren’t sure yet how late we can use our Peech Hotel room. There is a fitness club next door that I intend to use at some point to get a workout in and I think I would like to take in the Apartheid Museum that is an hour away in Soweto. That would require getting information about the status of the riots that have been going on in the townships, or at least were two weeks ago and determining if it is smart to go to Soweto right now. I would also need to get more Rand and it would take two hours of commute time. None of these things are enough to stop me, but I realize I am feeling a little lazy and just not that great.

MONDAY, JUNE 9

Linda in The Peech Hotel's computer room where she ended up spending a lot of her time

It is 8 a.m. on Monday; we should be landing about now in London, but we are still at the Peech Hotel in Johannesburg. I will explain in a few minutes.

After my last entry yesterday morning while sitting here at the Peech, Linda joined me for breakfast. Since I was not interested in doing much, we left the hotel to go for a walk to Melrose Arch, a development with stores, cafes and a hotel. Along the way, we stopped at a park where they were setting up for a family day event; it was Father's Day in South Africa.

It was warm out and nice and it was a great casual walk. We were gone two hours getting back to the hotel around noon. I went to our hotel room to read the guidebook about Johannesburg to see what else we might do. It was then I realized I really was not feeling well. I was so lethargic. I laid down and was about to doze off when Linda came bounding into the room with information about a nearby craft market. It was the last thing I felt like doing, but I couldn't just lay around and I definitely did not want Linda going by herself. On our morning walk, we got a good sense that even in this nice area of Johannesburg, it is not a place for a single white woman to be roaming.

The market was a mile and a half away; we decided to walk there and take a taxi back. When we got to the market I found myself noting where the bathrooms were. I was really beginning to not feel well. I was not enjoying as much as I should have been the active market; among other things there was music and dancers and all sorts of entertaining things.

I struggled through and finally after an hour or so I told Linda I had to get back to the hotel. It seemed like it took forever to get a cab and make the short drive. On the ride in the taxi, I told Linda I wondered if I had malaria. My symptoms were consistent with what little I knew about it.

I got back to our hotel room (which the Peech was kind enough to allow us to continue to use) and laid down. I was now feverish and felt terrible and eventually fell asleep. In the meantime, Linda got on the computer and researched malaria and talked with Sandy from Pulse Africa, the travel agent who arranged the safari portion of our trip. She and Linda came up with the plan that I would go to a clinic in London where Sandy had a connection and she knew would be well versed with malaria.

Linda woke me up at 5:30 p.m. so I could shower before our 6 p.m. ride to the airport for our flight to London. I wasn't feeling any better. Linda explained all the good work she had done while I dozed for two hours that afternoon and about the London clinic plan. As she described the symptoms for malaria that she had learned from her internet research, it was clear malaria was a real possibility. But then, so was the flu, or food poisoning. Sandy had stressed, as had others we had talked to the past two weeks, that early detection and treatment of malaria is critical. If you don't, you can become one of its victims.

I was not thinking clearly---a symptom consistent with malaria (and a lot of other things!)---and was illogically resisting Linda's suggestion that we not catch our flight, but rather stay in Johannesburg to see a doctor. Since Linda had been researching malaria and making calls, she was convinced the best place for malaria treatment was right here in Johannesburg—a place where the infliction is common. I stubbornly persist and we hop in the hotel's van for the ride to the Johannesburg Airport. As we neared the airport, my condition got considerably worse. Finally, I conceded Linda was right and we asked the driver to turn around and take us back to the Peech Hotel. He had just gotten turned around and was headed back to the hotel on the freeway, when I realized I was going to throw up.

This is Deja Vu all over again: I threw up from a moving van on our way home from Laos two years earlier.

I have my hand on the handle to slide the van door back as Linda is urgently telling the driver to get pulled over. He gets the message and starts negotiating traffic to get to the outside lane. I am trying to get the sliding door open even before we get stopped. He is saying, "Just a minute, just a minute" as he controls the van and fumbles for the power lock. Just a minute? I don't have a minute! I contain the first two "urps" with my mouth closed (pleasant, huh?) while I am ranking on the door handle. No way was I holding back "urp" number three---which erupted just as the van door started sliding back. About half the stuff made it outside the van. I pretty well covered the guard rail, but that is a huge improvement because in Laos I came within feet of splattering school children walking alongside the road. We sat there for a moment as I recovered and made sure I had no more to offer. Checking out the mess, I noted that the tomatoes I had for breakfast looked a lot more appealing when I ate them.

After vomiting I felt much better and I made the ride back to the Peech just fine. I immediately crawled into bed and laid there feverishly all night. This morning I woke up feeling just fine. Linda has arranged for a "Doctor on Call" to come see me here at the hotel. Since I feel better, I doubt I have malaria, but it is better to be safe. We have Sandy working on arranging new flights for us to get home.

Linda had telephoned Britt to let her know we would not be coming home to Seattle when planned. We asked her to let Dennis know as well, but not to alarm anyone. So, I just now used the Peech Hotel's computer to get this quick note off to Dennis:

> ***JOHANNESBURG, SOUTH AFRICA***
> ***Subject: On our way home***
>
> *Dennis,*
>
> *I think Britt got a message off to you so you know we are delayed getting home....haven't been able to re-book flights yet so not sure when.*
>
> *We actually did a U-turn when we got to the airport last night to catch our flight. Minutes after the U-turn, the driver had to pull over so I could throw up (Laos all over again...throwing up from a moving van taking us to the airport for the trip home!).*
>
> *I don't think that flu alone would have prevented me from getting on the flight. The concern is that I have Malaria and I*

am thinking I can get better treatment for Malaria here in Johannesburg than elsewhere. I have a doctor coming to see me at the hotel here in an hour, but the fact that I feel better today makes malaria less likely. At least that is what I am hoping. Never heard any good stories about malaria!

For obvious reasons I didn't want Malaria mentioned to anyone so Britt didn't mention it in her email.

I will keep you informed!

Gary

TUESDAY, JUNE 10

On our flight home from London---malaria free!

No malaria---nice relief!

The local doctor Linda arranged came to see me yesterday morning at the Peech Hotel, took my blood and looked me over. Around 1:30 p.m., an hour and a half later than we expected, we got the word that the blood test results were negative for malaria. I have never heard any good stories about malaria, so I was happy to hear that.

Linda and I decided it made no sense to try to get new flights through the Alaska Airlines Partner desk until we knew for sure I would be able to leave. The doctor had told us there was a chance I could be hospitalized if the test results came back positive. So, in the meantime, we checked out nearby hotels since the Peech was full and couldn't accommodate us if we needed to stay. I walked down the street to a place to purchase more airtime for our cell phone for calling airlines and hotels and to be sure I knew where a nearby ATM was in case we had to spend another night or two.

Except for an aching stomach and aching muscles everywhere, I felt pretty good. No fever, no nausea, nothing.

It turned out that our anxiety over waiting longer than we expected for my lab tests came back was not justified since the Alaska Airline reservation line didn't open until 2:00 p.m. (South Africa time). Having the word from the doctor that I was okay, we dialed the Alaska Air number at 1:59 p.m. and got through immediately. Within eleven minutes we had reservations all the way through to Seattle in the same class and same flight numbers as the flight we missed the night before. It was amazing, and totally unexpected! Apparently, when using air miles, you have to make reservations 330 days in advance---or just one day---if you want to find availability.

With our flights arranged we booked a taxi to the airport at 4 p.m. to avoid the horrendous Johannesburg traffic (our flight wouldn't leave until 9 p.m.), we went in to the Peech's bistro around 2:30 p.m. for a late lunch; my first meal since the morning before!

Now that we knew what our plan was, I fired off a quick group email home:

> ***JOHANNESBURG, SOUTH AFRICA***
> ***Subject: On our way home***
>
> *Hi everyone,*
>
> *Some of you got the word that we were delayed getting home. Everything is ok, and we will be home at around 5 pm tomorrow, Tuesday.*
>
> *Talk to you soon!*
>
> *Gary*

They won't forget us soon at the Peech Hotel. Linda normally utilizes a hotel's staff to the max anyway, but after accommodating us for late checkout the day before when I was sick, me hurling all over the inside of the hotel's van, re-checking in and then hanging around their small lobby all day yesterday and today, the doctor coming and going (three different times), faxes coming in for the doctor and Sandy from Pulse Africa calling several times to communicate with us---they won't know what to do with themselves without us! Even the hotel owner, James, was involved. We tipped everyone well and I made a point of making sure James knew how awesome his staff had been and how much we appreciated it.

We will also need to consider doing something special for Sandy. True, her company, Pulse Africa, likely made good money off our bookings through them, but her concern and attentiveness went well beyond all of that. She was very helpful.

I have been writing from British Airline's "arrival" lounge in Terminal 5 of Heathrow airport. Our plan was to go into London after we freshened up, so we went through immigration/customs and then came into the "arrival" lounge. I have wondered why an airline has an "arrival" lounge; it has computers, showers (lots of them), massages and meals. It is a very busy place; people must use it after long flights to shower or eat before leaving the airport to go into London for their business, or I suppose like us for a day-trip before coming back to the airport to depart again. Had we not planned on the day-trip, we would have gone straight to our departure terminal (Terminal 4) and used the airline's "departure" lounge there. In any event, we are here in the "arrival" lounge and enjoying it!

We have decided not to go into London; it isn't worth it. We would have only two hours once we got downtown and the express subway (thirty minutes to downtown) costs 15 pounds each way per person. That is 60 pounds or $120 US! We should have pre-arranged to meet Melinda and/or James (our London friends from Belize) for tea or lunch. That would have been fun.

Both Linda and I showered here at the "arrivals" lounge. It felt really good, but there is something wrong about putting on the same clothes you slept in the night before. Yes, I slept a full 6½ hours during last night's 11-hour flight from Johannesburg. Nothing like a little sickness to give you a good night's sleep! I had the change of clothes thing all figured out two days ago when we first tried to leave Johannesburg, but throwing up all over one set of clothes put a stinky wrinkle in those plans.

To catch our 3:00 p.m. flight to Seattle, we will take a 25-minute bus ride around the airport to Terminal 4 and will go through immigration and security there. We will arrive 5 p.m. Seattle time and sweet Britt will pick us up at SeaTac. Journey over.

Let me summarize this trip a little:

On the wildlife side, it is impossible to identify a favorite. Seeing the African Wild Dogs was an unexpected surprise. Hunted almost to extinction, they are the most efficient hunters of all the predators; it is no wonder after witnessing the wildlife films of a pack of them hunting their quarry. And yet, they look like your pet dog.

Any image of African landscape without a giraffe is missing a big piece. Their graceful, loping movement is an integral part of my image of an African vista. I think both Linda and I favor them; I hope the carved, wooden ones we bought make it home unbroken.

The sinewy, stealthy movements of the leopard and its remarkably beautiful and unique coat make it a stand-out.

The lazy, fear-nothing attitude of the lion naturally stems from the fact it is the king of the jungle. It also makes you think---for just a moment---that you could safely hop out of the landie, lay down next to one and get no reaction from the lethal cat but a yawn.

The hippo, killer of more humans than any other animal in Africa, is a curiosity. Inherently ugly, its head is so massive he has trouble raising it; he can't swim, but spends most of his time in the water; he has massive teeth and jaws, yet eats grass; he weighs several tons, has short, stubby lets, yet can run 20 MPH; he is nervous and skittish, yet aggressive and mean.

The kindly intelligent elephant is the most feared of all of Africa's creatures by villagers. Elephants are numerous and stumbling into the path of a breeding herd, on foot or vehicle, can quickly prove fatal. We heard several stories about landies with holes in radiators, or rolled over by angry female elephants. And yet, when you are around them in a controlled situation, you sense their intelligence and nurturing nature.

The bird life of Africa never gets enough mention. The remarkably colorful birds are too numerous to mention.

Of the places we stayed in Botswana and Zambia, I think I give the edge to Chongwe River Camp, it had the best "tents" and most active camp grounds, even though its game viewing was less varied. The Tafika Camp is a close second. But really, both camps were top-notch and nearly a toss-up.

The low-light of the camps was the walking camp, Chikoko Bush Camp. It was the one I looked forward to the most, but now I know that walking safaris are much more limited than driving safaris. Not only in terms of the amount of ground you can cover, but you can get much closer to the wildlife in a landie; much closer than you would ever want to on foot! The camp and the tent at Chikoko was awesome; entirely open, dirt floors, no running water---very cool.

In the Okavango, I preferred Chief's Camp over Baines Camp. Part of this is because I really liked our guide, Jonathan, at Chief's. The major difference, though, was Baines Camp was too far from the wildlife; we would typically have a 45-minute bouncing drive to get to good game viewing. Although it is true, it was at Baines where the lion walked through the camp, and I loved sleeping outdoors at Baines.

We had awesome guides. Even the one (Ben) who I thought was a bull-shitter managed to overcome my skepticism eventually. And, without exception, the camp managers and owners were just super. Storm was hot and John Coppinger a celebrity (featured in two separate airline magazine articles, just that I happened to see), but they were all intelligent, accommodating and fun to be around.

I have to remember to thank Sandy from Pulse Africa. She paid for my micro-flight with John at Tafika since she screwed up the Zimbabwe portion of our trip.

I did not have great expectations of South Africa, but it really enthralled me. I really enjoyed that portion of our trip. Cape Town is a wonderful city.

We have learned, from talking to other travelers on this trip, that eastern South Africa, Lesotho and the beaches and islands of Mozambique would be great travel options for the future. Also, Malawi and Namibia. A drive from Windhoek, Namibia through Zambia into Malawi would be a great road adventure, although maybe a lot of time in a landie. Something to figure out another day.

Fantasizing about future trips is not meant to take anything away from this one. It was marvelous, simply marvelous. I am really glad it didn't end with malaria!

Until next time....

Gary

POST-TRIP EMAIL

The following is the email I sent to Pulse Africa reporting on our trip after we returned home to Seattle:

PULSE AFRICA
Subject: Our African Adventure

Sandy & Robynne,

I am sorry this has taken so long to get around to. I wanted to give you our feedback on the trip you arranged for us, which was, in order:

- *Chief's Camp*
- *Baines Camp*
- *Tongabezi*
- *Chongwe River Camp*
- *Chikoko Bush Camp*
- *Tafika Camp*

We stayed three nights at each location, except Chikoko (1 night) and Tafika (2 nights).

First, everything was GREAT! So please remember that the following comments fit into the categories of nuances and personal tastes. I think you will find that most of our impressions will merely reinforce things you already know and had told us.

Our "Best Camp of the Trip" award goes to Chongwe River Camp; Tafika was a close second. The Okavango Camps were tied for third and Chikoko was last. Had we been that scientific about it, there would not have been many "points" separating any of these camps, trust me. They were all great, although Linda might not agree with that assessment regarding Chikoko. Here is a little more detail:

- ***Chongwe River Camp*** *had just the right mix of comfort and the rustic feel of the bush. Its unfenced and active camp grounds allowed for hippos, elephants and other animals to roam within meters of our tent---which they did. We will* *forever remember the "wheeze-snort-snort-snort" of the hippos lurking in the river out our tent's front flap (Linda is tired of hearing my rendition). Chongwe's tents were the most "safari appropriate" of our trip; comfortable and nice, yet they were simply tents with nothing but the netted side drapes between you and the hippos as they thumped by on their nightly walk inland to forage. Having the water activities was a nice variation from the land-based game drives as well.*

- ***Tafika** is an awesome camp. The Coppingers' presence makes a noticeable difference in the organization and personality of the camp. The accommodations were similar to, but not as unique as, Chongwe's. The ease and diversity of game viewing at Tafika was better than Chongwe's.*

- *We loved **Chief's and Baines Camps**, but in hindsight, would have done only one of these two camps, probably Chief's, substituting Baines for three nights in, perhaps Magkadigkadi, to get a flavor of the Kalahari Desert. We slightly preferred Chief's Camp because of the ease of game-viewing; at Baines we had to drive over the same track 45 minutes each drive get to game, which wasn't the case at Chief's. Of course, both camps are dramatically affected by the seasonal water levels, so this may change at different times, but higher water levels would make Baines much less desirable. The accommodations at both camps were very nice. At Baines, I LOVED rolling my bed onto the exterior deck each night to sleep under the stars, although I was surprised I was the only one in the camp to do so.*

- ***Chikoko Bush Camp** was a minor disappointment. Not because it failed, but because my expectations were out of line. As you might remember, I was looking forward to a bush camp; its isolation, ruggedness and the fact that it was different. I enjoyed the walking safaris because they were unique and new to me. But having now done them, I am not much inspired to do so again. After days of bouncing around in landies and confined to tents, the walking exercise felt great, but you cover so much more ground, see more animals and see them more closely from a landie. I loved the lack of electricity and running water, the open tents and dirt floors,* *but it wasn't so much Linda's cup of tea. She was a champ and tolerated it, but was too fearful to participate in the walking safaris.*

Without exception, the flights and ground transfers were organized, on time and supported by helpful, friendly staff. The staffs of all the camps and Tongabezi were simply awesome. With the exception of one guide at Baines, who substituted for a day for the regular guide who was ill, the guides were exceptional throughout.

The report card on ***Pulse Africa*** *is flawless. Sure, there was the "blonde moment" (Sandy's words, not mine) resulting in our not getting into Zimbabwe, but your acknowledgement of that and arranging for me the micro-flight with John Coppinger was much appreciated. Not enough can be said about how Sandy went well beyond any measure of what could reasonably be expected in helping Linda deal with my illness in Johannesburg. Sandy seemed to understand our anxiety of dealing, in a foreign country, with the possibility of malaria, a sickness which is to us unfamiliar and scary. And God knows I wasn't in any position to be thinking straight! So, a HUGE thank you to Sandy for her over-the-top support during that time.*

When I talked about sending this to you, I thought it would be more helpful than it has turned out. I guess when everything is good, there isn't much to be learned from me saying so---except that maybe you shouldn't change anything!

Thanks to you we had an incredible first experience in Africa. It exceeded our high expectations. You will likely be hearing from various friends of ours over the next few months and years. We know you will do for them what you did for us!

Gary Brown (and Linda Griffin)

www.ingramcontent.com/pod-product-compliance
Ingram Content Group UK Ltd.
Pitfield, Milton Keynes, MK11 3LW, UK
UKHW041943190726
13854UKWH00004B/1756